THE STORY OF PEACE AND WAR

The Story of
PEACE and WAR

Thomas Franklin

by ~~TOM~~ GALT

With Illustrations by ERIK BLEGVAD

New York:

THOMAS Y. CROWELL COMPANY

PRINTED IN THE UNITED STATES OF AMERICA
BY THE VAIL-BALLOU PRESS, INC., BINGHAMTON, N. Y.

Table of Contents

Table of Contents

1. *War Is Your Problem*

WE ALREADY know how to stop wars. The world has a method for preventing them entirely.

This book will show what the method is and how it has been growing.

Think for a minute, the difference peace will make to you, if we can get it.

Guns, tanks, fighter planes, bullets, atom bombs, and

pay for soldiers of the United States in 1951 cost sixty billion dollars.

That is four hundred dollars from each person. Can you think of anything you would like to do with your four hundred dollars if it were not spent on weapons?

How much is that from your whole family? If you have a father and mother and one brother or a sister, multiply by four. That makes sixteen hundred dollars from your family every year. What would you like to do with that money?

In World War II millions of houses were destroyed. Ships were sunk. Railroad trains were shot up. Factories, warehouses, and stores full of clothing, food, and other merchandise were burned and bombed.

New things had to be made and bought to replace most of them. These new things cost hundreds of billions of dollars.

All this money was taken away from people—including your family. It is money that could buy a new bicycle, a trip to the country or to the city, a violin, an automobile.

And if we have another world war, an atom bomb may burst like a man-made sun much too close to you. It may burn you painfully, or push you so hard against a building or sidewalk that it will break your arms and legs, or knock down the bricks of a house or store on top of you. It may kill your mother or father or your friends. It may blast out your house—and also most of your city.

. As you walk about among the smoking heaps of brick and charred wood next day, trying to see where the streets used to be, you may find that it has burned the grocery stores and overturned the grocers' trucks and the trains, so that you may not be able to get food.

What are we going to do about this? What way is there to stop wars?

Let's not dream of an impossible answer. Let's look at the world and see what method people really have.

2. *The First Wars and the First Leagues*

WHEN DID wars begin? Among wild animals?

The word *war* means a group of men or animals fighting against another group of men or animals of the same species. Wild animals don't usually do that.

Lions kill antelopes, but that is not war; it is only their way of going to market for food. If a large group of lions attacked another large group of lions and fought till many were killed, that would be war. But lions don't. Sometimes two lions fight, but that is not war, and besides they rarely kill each other. Foxes kill chickens, but they don't often kill each other.

Our ancestors, the great apes, were more quarrelsome than lions or foxes. But even when apes fought they only shouted and bit and scratched till one drove the other away. They seldom killed each other.

However, sometimes a whole family of apes attacked another family. This was war—though not very destructive. They chased each other among the trees. As they could move very fast, their battles consisted of sudden rushes and a great deal of climbing and jumping. Almost all the losing side usually ran away.

Certainly the apes invented war.

Primitive people continued to fight like that. Tree dwellers and cave men had many small quarrels, one family against another.

Later some families tried to live near each other in huts of twigs and mud, making a village or small tribe. At first they did not know how to get along together.

For example, a man chased a rabbit for a long time in the hot sunlight, running as hard as he could. He was hungry and wanted the meat. At the bend of the river he was just about to hit the animal with a stone.

But at that moment another man, who had been hiding there all morning behind a bush, hungrily waiting for some rabbit to come along, threw his spear and got it.

Each man claimed the rabbit. So they fought with spears and stone axes. When they staggered back to the village both were wounded and dying. Each man's brothers and sons took his side. A little war began.

Fighting families drove one another away and broke up the village.

In order to live together the tribe needed a system for keeping peace. So they began to follow chiefs. And they began to believe in taboos, which said a family must not fight for revenge against other men of the same village. Instead, when someone had killed his neighbor, the whole village must join in a big religious ceremony and work off their feelings by dancing and praying. This was healthier than a war between two families.

It took mankind thousands of years even to learn how a number of families could live together in one village.

They learned that in order to keep peace between families, the village must have chiefs and it must have customs and laws. This was *government*. Without government there was no peace. With government, peace became possible.

However, as soon as people learned how to live together in villages or tribes, one tribe began to fight against another.

Usually this meant only a little squabbling. A "war party" of six or eight young men would sneak to an-

other tribe's camp at night and try to steal a few rein-
deer or sheep or women. This adventure was very exciting because it was dangerous, for sometimes some of
the men were killed.

Less often the braves of a whole tribe would go out
against another tribe.

Why did they do that? For two main reasons.

Sometimes the other tribe's hunting grounds seemed
better or their fields looked greener. A hothead would
start the trouble by shouting, "Why should we have
poorer fields than those dirty people have? It's not fair!
To arms, men! Drive them away!"

Or sometimes a chief felt uneasy because his government was weak and the families in his tribe were quarreling with each other too much. So he would try to persuade them to start a war. War was useful to the chief.
In the excitement of preparing for battle, family quarrels were forgotten, and the people were more willing to
obey him.

In order to start the mischief the warriors would
gather around a campfire and try to remember (or invent) crimes committed by the other tribe. A man
would say, "They killed my cousin while he was pick-
ing berries!" Someone else would say, "They killed
a deer that belonged to me!" One or two crimes were not
enough to overcome the men's reluctance to slaughter
other men. The warriors had to accuse their enemy of
many outrages. Always the war could not begin until

the whole tribe found enough excuses for saying, "The other tribe has done wrong to us! We must fight to defend our honor!"

In the battle they did a great deal of shouting. Some heroes from one tribe fought single combats against heroes from the other tribe. The common warriors made sudden rushes to try to take prisoners. Only a few men were killed.

But mankind is restless, always developing new methods. Things never go on being done the same way.

People learned how to live in larger towns. They also learned how to organize larger groups of warriors. Battles began to be bigger and more effectively managed, so that more men were killed.

In 500 B.C. the Greek, Persian, and Egyptian armies used to swarm out onto a battlefield—tens of thousands of men—running around, yelling, and shooting arrows. Each man fought with sword or spears as he thought best.

Then King Philip of Macedon in 350 B.C. introduced military discipline. He trained his soldiers, taught them to parade, invented right face, left face, forward march, to-the-rear march, squads right, squads left! And he paid the men wages.

The first time he marched his disciplined army in parade formation into battle against a swarm of barbarian Scythians the result was astonishing.

The barbarians, who had been victorious in many battles, made a semicircle about two miles long, keeping away from Philip's men, waiting for him to begin. When it looked as though he would attack at the center of their semicircle, most of the barbarians rushed there to be ahead of the marching column and try to stop it.

The king stood in a chariot to watch. He called, "Squads right!" This order was repeated by stentors, who had loud voices. His whole army marched to the right.

The barbarians, taken by surprise, swarmed over to that end of their line. But just before his soldiers reached them, the king commanded, "To the rear— march!"

His army, their swords, shields, and helmets clanking and glistening in the sunlight, worked like a machine. They marched in the opposite direction, leaving the bulk of the enemy directly behind them. His army attacked where the enemy were weakest, then wheeled about and chewed up another thin spot in their line.

When the barbarians charged, King Philip gave commands and quickly surrounded most of them. Thousands were slaughtered. Those who broke through ran away, believing they had been attacked by a god.

Philip's new army was terribly effective everywhere he used it. He conquered most of Greece.

His son, Alexander the Great, was a young athlete. He had blond hair, a handsome face, powerful shoulders, a slim waist, and almost no human feelings at all. He inherited the army and immediately began to use it. He conquered an enormous empire with it: all of Greece, Egypt, Persia.

The new army was expensive, because the soldiers had to be trained and paid. It was also destructive. It was so efficient that it burned and destroyed dozens of cities.

Alexander fought all the way to India. There he asked five philosophers, "What is the worst thing in the world?"

They replied, "Alexander is. Because he has killed so many people."

If they could have read the future they would have seen that Alexander's army was only a small beginning. Armies were going to go right on growing more and more expensive and more and more destructive.

At the same time that Philip and Alexander were making such advances in the techniques of war, the ancient Greeks also made one of the first important experiments with a method for keeping peace.

They lived in several dozen city-states. Each of these cities fought many wars. They fought foreign nations. They also fought each other. For a short time Philip and Alexander ruled them all but could not entirely stop their fighting. As soon as Alexander died, most of the Greek cities began to fight each other freely again. Athens and Sparta ended by destroying one another almost entirely.

This is not surprising, as these city-states were completely independent. And independent states are sovereign. They act like sovereigns—that is, like kings. Often they act like very selfish, haughty, quarrelsome sovereigns.

But when any two cities of the Achaean League had a dispute, they did not fight, as other Greek cities did. The Achaean cities sent lawyers and witnesses to their council's meeting place. The lawyers argued. The witnesses gave the facts. The councilors asked questions.

Then the councilors talked about possible settlements. One city must pay the other some money or give up some land or change its laws so as to stop annoying the other.

When the councilors voted a decision, it had to be obeyed. Why? Because if any city tried to disobey, the whole army of the league, led by the president, marched to that city, arrested its officials, tried them in court, and punished those who had been guilty of disobedience.

This Achaean League consisted of a dozen small Greek city-states.

The voters of each city got together and elected ten councilors. These men from the twelve cities (120 men) were the league council. They dressed themselves in fine linen robes and sat together in the morning sunlight in a round open-air court with five rows of curved stone benches.

The league also had a popular assembly. Twice each year the voters—as many of the voters in the twelve cities as were able to get away for a few days from their farms or businesses—went to the capital and sat in a large field. This was the league's parliament or congress.

They made laws, decided what taxes should be collected, managed the league army, and made one kind of money for the whole league.

The Achaean League was able to keep peace among its member cities because each city had given up some of its right to act like a haughty sovereign.

But the Achaean League fought against outsiders. Unfortunately it fought a long war against another league (the Aetolian, which was very much like it). The two weakened each other badly, until the Romans came (in 146 B.C.) and conquered both.

However, the Achaean League had lasted about 130 years. It showed us a method by which states or nations can work together and not fight each other.

The method works even among people who, in ideas and habits, are extremely different from the ancient Greeks.

In America the Iroquois were farmers. They also were great fighters. They moved into what is now New

York State and drove out the other Indians who had been there.

But also the five Iroquois tribes fought one another. For a while farming became almost impossible. An Indian man or woman could not go into the fields without danger of being attacked by some war party of enemy braves.

Hiawatha was the chief of a large family in one of the Iroquois tribes. He had grown up in this trouble. He saw that it was wasteful and unnecessary. So he thought out a rough outline of a scheme for making his people safe.

The council of family chiefs of his Onondaga tribe met around the campfire in their largest village. Hiawatha stood up. He was tall, keen eyed, and quick of speech. He said excitedly, "Let us try to join with the rest of the Iroquois in a Great Peace League."

The principal chief, Atortaho, was a haughty and clever leader. He stood up next. Shaking his feather plumes, he made fun of the scheme. "Dreamers talk of peace. Wise men sharpen their weapons."

Most of the councilors agreed with Atortaho.

Hiawatha went home angry and disappointed. But he accepted the challenge of the other men's laughter. Raising his chin stubbornly, he set out alone to prove that the league could be made.

He walked over the forested hills to a small village of the enemy Oneidas. There he entered the hut of the local chief, Dekanawida, a large, slow, dark man, known as a maker of songs.

This man listened in silence for a long time, then became enthusiastic about the scheme. He helped to improve it and made it more definite.

He spoke at a meeting of chiefs. He was a good speaker. By his graphic description of the advantages of a league, he won over the council of his whole nation.

Hiawatha and Dekanawida then traveled hopefully together to the Cayugas. These were easily persuaded. The council of the Cayugas even worked out a neat way to win Hiawatha's own people, the Onondagas, whose chief, Atortaho, had been the first to laugh at the scheme. The Onondagas were important, as they were the largest nation of the Iroquois. So the planners decided to ask Atortaho to be the head of the whole new league.

When Hiawatha marched home triumphantly, bringing chiefs from the two tribes he had won over, his own people took his scheme much more seriously than before.

Atortaho heard he was to be the head of it. He began to look very dignified and soon decided the scheme was good. He himself undertook to persuade the Senecas and the Mohawks.

Thousands of braves gathered for the great ceremony of beginning the League of the Five Nations. Delegates from all the tribes dug up a large tree. Hiawatha's new friend called out loudly, "I, Dekanawida, and the confederate lords now uproot this tallest pine tree and into the cavity thereby made we cast all weapons of war. Into the depths of the earth, down into the deep under-earth currents of water flowing into unknown regions, we cast all weapons of strife. We bury them from sight forever and plant again the tree. Thus shall a Great Peace be established, and hostilities shall no longer be known between the Five Nations, but only peace to a united people."

A united people. That is the whole point. When people are united, they don't fight each other.

The league was managed by a council of representatives of the tribes. The Onondagas, being the largest, sent fourteen representatives. The other tribes sent nine each, or eight, according to their size. These representatives were nominated by the noblest women of each tribe, and voted on by the councils of chiefs (one chief for each family) in the villages.

The league council met frequently. Sitting in a circle round a fire, they made laws for all matters that concerned the whole league—leaving local problems to the local councils.

Murder was considered a league affair and was punished by the league council. The council received ambassadors from outside tribes, sometimes made treaties of peace with them, sometimes declared war against them. The league conquered three or four other tribes, made them colonies, and the council governed them.

One large tribe (the Tuscarora of what is now North Carolina) was admitted to full membership, so that the league became the Six Nations.

For two hundred years the league succeeded in preventing any major war among its members. It was not perfect. The young braves, who were not represented on the council, often got out of control and started small fights. But the council always managed to stop them so there were no battles between the tribes.

However, the league fought against its neighbors. It fought against the white men more firmly than any other group of Indians in North America. In these wars the Six Nations were greatly weakened and lost most of their land.

But the league still exists. In 1950 six representatives visited the new United Nations buildings in New York. They understood what they were looking at, because their league had been a beginning of the same system that the U.N. is trying to use for the whole world.

3. *Medieval Wars and Peace Plans*

DURING THE Middle Ages, Europe was covered heavily with forests. Men with axes cleared a space among the trees and sheltered themselves in a small fortified town or a castle surrounded by little huts. To travel to another place where people lived you had to walk or ride on a narrow path through the forest. Those trips were dangerous. Bears and wolves lurked in the forest, and desperate outlaws and brigands made a trip more perilous.

Government was very crude. Each village or castle was ruled by its lord, and if you were in it you had to obey him. Theoretically he obeyed the duke or count or baron above him. In fact, sometimes he obeyed, sometimes not. A few castles belonged to a duke, another half dozen to an earl or count. A baron might own twenty villages.

The king was richer. He owned a couple of dozen castles and several towns, each ruled by a nobleman. With pluck the king could make most of them obey him. He also was supposed to make his dukes, earls, counts, and barons obey him, but that was more difficult. They all had soldiers of their own. They frequently made war against one another, and the king could not stop them. Whenever they felt like it, they even made war against him.

The Middle Ages was the time of personal wars. A baron wanted to own a few more castles. So he attacked his neighbor. If the baron won, he got money from the farmers he had conquered, and more people had to obey him. Nowadays a businessman expands his company so that he can have more money and more people taking orders from him. In the Middle Ages a man fought personal wars for that purpose.

The knights who did the actual fighting were men who had nothing else to do. They were bored. Also, whenever they captured a town they used to steal everything they could find in it: money, jewels, furniture, even pots and pans. So fighting was a way of earning a living.

But this system of governing—called the *feudal system*—was weak and wasteful. Gradually people learned how to organize larger governments. Then the little duchies and earldoms and counties and baronies were put together and made bigger.

In 1066 William the Conqueror conquered England and forced the whole country to be one nation. He made himself the real ruler of it.

Gradually the kings of France got better control of their noblemen. Joan of Arc helped make her country become one nation.

In 1492 the parts of Spain joined and became one nation. By then most of the little pieces of Europe had grown together into nations. (But not Germany and Italy, which remained in fragments for another 350 years.)

All over the world the same thing was happening—in China, India, Russia. Feudal baronies and small kingdoms were conquering one another, joining together to become large nations.

At the same time knights got better and better armor. They fought on horseback with long swords and spears. The armor and horses were expensive. War cost more than it ever had before.

Then the English organized an army of trained and

disciplined longbowmen. They could shoot down the horses and pierce the chinks of the armor without letting the knights get near enough to do anything. It looked as though war would be cheap, because bows and arrows did not cost much.

But the French and Germans organized longbowmen, too. And these soldiers had to be paid.

And other weapons were made. Just before 1300 somebody brought from China the idea of making gunpowder. Men began to build small cannons. Immediately cannon spread all over Europe. An English army used them against the Scots in 1327. A French army fired them at the Flemish soldiers in 1338.

The first cannons were shot off only to begin a battle. As soon as your men had rushed in to fight, you could not shoot any more at the enemy without hitting some of your own soldiers, too.

Soon after 1400 a hand gun (the harquebus) was invented. A man fired it by poking a burning stick into it. In 1476 it acquired a trigger. Then soldiers began to use it in war.

Larger armies used these new weapons. In the twelfth century only eighty thousand men had been killed in battles in Europe; in the fifteenth century over five hundred thousand.

These large armies were even more expensive than the knights had been. And they did far more damage, looting towns, burning farms.

With so much fighting going on, naturally people began to wonder—wasn't there some method for keeping peace?

A few scholars read Greek history and wagged their heads over the Achaean League. They frowned and asked one another, "Couldn't we keep peace by a European league?"

The first man to write this bold idea in a book was a French lawyer, Pierre Dubois. He was a successful politician, an adviser to barons, dukes, and kings. He talked with rulers and with scholars all over Europe. He found that many of them were saying the same thing about a European league. So in the year 1306 he wrote the plan in a book, *On the Recovery of the Holy Land.*

The Pope, he wrote, should invite the kings and sovereign princes and highest cardinals and bishops to meet together. The Pope would be the president of this Council of Europe.

They would make laws for Europe. Together they would pay for an army to drive the Mohammedans out of the Holy Land.

Any quarrel between two sovereigns would be settled by an international court. Each of the two quarreling rulers would appoint three judges. The Council of Europe would appoint three more.

If any sovereign started a war or refused to obey a decision of the court, all the others must attack his country.

This plan was read and talked about. The scribes made many copies. Many people liked it.

But every sovereign in Europe turned it down. Every king or prince refused to join any council or international court whose decisions he would have to obey.

Of course every king refused! A sovereign believed that he could always do as he pleased. Obey the majority in a council full of kings? Not he!

Each of the democratic cities of the Achaean League had given up some of its independent sovereignty to the league. Then the voters of the cities voted in the league. But no king or prince in Europe in 1306 was willing to give up any of his independence. So they went on fighting, and their wars became worse and worse.

Four years later, in 1310, the famous poet Dante wrote a book, *Of Monarchy*. It said that for the sake of peace there should be one king to rule all Europe, making it one nation. This sounded logical. If the kings won't get together, let's have only one king.

But how well would it work actually?

Five centuries later it was tried by Napoleon. It was tried again in 1944 by Hitler, who conquered all of Europe. And what happened? Evidently it is not a good plan. When one man gets that much power, he goes crazy. He attacks one country after another and makes slaves of its people.

George Podiebrad, king of Bohemia (which we now call Czechoslovakia), tried to rescue what was good in

Pierre Dubois' old plan and improve it. In 1464 he wrote to all the sovereigns of Europe, asking them to send ambassadors to meet together as a council. This council would appoint the judges of an international court.

The Pope did not like this plan, which left him out. Two years later he excommunicated George.

Erasmus, the witty Dutch scholar, wrote *A Complaint of Peace* in 1514, stressing the need for an international court to arbitrate disputes between sovereigns. Wouldn't it be better to settle quarrels by talk than by killing people? He wrote, "One can hardly imagine an unfavorable peace that would not be better than the most favorable war."

Meanwhile—as the scholars were writing plans and the sovereigns were fighting wars—a group of cities in Germany proved once again that we do know how to keep peace, provided we use the right method.

These cities had a sort of businessmen's democracy. The masters of all the little shoemaking shops had a guild and elected their guild president, vice-president, and treasurer. The masters of the bakeries had a bakers' guild. And there were a brewers' guild, a weavers' guild, a goldsmiths' guild, one for every trade.

In each city the presidents, vice-presidents, and treasurers of all the guilds met together and elected the mayor of the city.

By the year 1200 these German cities were beginning to buy cloth, iron, copper, food, beer, and other goods from one another. But they lost many cargoes to pirates on the seas and rivers and to brigands in the forests.

Three cities joined together in 1219 and sent armed ships to clear the pirates off the Elbe River. Two years later Hamburg and Lübeck signed a treaty for mutual defense against brigands. Soon these cities all joined together, and others came in with them, forming a hanse. (*Hanse* means *league,* and we call them the Hanseatic League.)

By 1260, when the first assembly (Hansetag) met at Lübeck, the league already had an organized government, with an army, a navy, and a system of taxes.

About once every three years the member cities sent delegates to the assembly, usually at Lübeck. The delegates, wealthy officers of guilds, came dressed in fine suits of embroidered red and brown cloth trimmed with fur. The Guildhall, where they met, was decorated with designs in gold and scarlet like a small palace. They discussed league business. Decisions were made by majority vote.

The assembly also arbitrated disputes between the cities. When anyone broke the league's rules about manufacturing or trade, they punished him, making him pay a fine. When a whole city disobeyed, the league boycotted it.

The purposes of the league were to keep the peace, to

protect business from pirates and brigands, and to improve commerce. The league went into the shipping business, built hundreds of ships, and made a great deal of money. It built canals and roads connecting all the member cities. Patient horses on the long tow paths among the wheat fields pulled the slow barges. Sailors with tar in their hair spread the large sails of the cargo ships over the waves of the Baltic and the North Sea.

More and more cities joined, until seventy-two were members, including all the important ones in northern Germany. They did not give up very much of their independent sovereignty to the league. In their local political affairs they remained entirely free. But they gave to the league most rights connected with business and foreign affairs.

The league had a navy with over twelve thousand armed men. The league made treaties with England and other countries to increase commerce. It had offices, warehouses, and wharves in 164 cities, including Novgorod, London, Marseilles. It made war on Denmark and Norway and beat them. The league army removed the king from the throne of Sweden and put on another king.

But nothing goes on the same forever.

For nearly four hundred years the league was successful. Then strong businesses grew up in other countries. The league had become selfish. It demanded special privileges in England (the right to export goods without paying tariffs) but would not give any such privileges to Englishmen in the Hanse towns. Queen Elizabeth at last angrily took away all its privileges in England.

The league became old-fashioned. One by one its members slipped away. By 1650 only three remained. They clung together till 1810, when Napoleon put an end to the overproud Hanseatic League.

It had acted out the same old story which we have seen in ancient Greece and with the Six Nations of the Iroquois Indians. The league could keep peace among its members, but it fought against outsiders.

4. *Diplomacy*

BY THE year 1500 large groups of Europeans, Asiatics, and American Indians had joined together to form nations. This raised the question: How were these nations to get along with one another? How could they meet and talk, or sell food, spices, iron, or jewels to each other?

It was not going to be easy. Every nation was ruled by a sovereign. And he thought he could do as he pleased.

What must happen when a dozen kings lived that way in Europe? Imagine a dozen proud people trying to play baseball when none would obey any rules. How long would it be before they would begin fighting?

And those kings were dangerous. Their armies had become larger. Weapons and techniques of killing had been made more effective.

In the time of ancient Greece and Egypt and Persia there had been no regular relations between one country and another. Once every few years the Pharoah of Egypt would send a messenger to Athens. The messenger would walk up the road from the beach, preceded by two heralds blowing horns. Always he would carry either a white flag or some other emblem to show that he came to parley, not to fight.

The flag of truce was usually respected, so that after his conversation he was allowed to go home again.

Between such visits the ruler of any country was out of touch with the rulers of the other countries.

When a merchant wanted to travel abroad, he paid some men with swords to go along and protect him. Even so, he took his chances.

Foreign traders who stayed in Athens had almost no rights. Their own countries would not try to help them. Some lived there all their lives. But they were at the mercy of the rulers of Athens, who actually treated them rather badly.

In the Middle Ages a new method began, a new way for a country to get along with others. This method is diplomacy.

One little independent state in Italy sent an ambassador to live at the capital of another state. Not merely to visit for a few days, but to live there. The senate of his town paid him a salary and also hired a man on horseback (a courier) to carry letters to him every week or two and bring letters back.

This was very useful. The ambassador hung around and got to know people in the foreign capital where he lived. He had lunch with a bishop, tea with a wealthy businessman, dinner with the local ruler's nephew (a conceited fellow with curly yellow hair and gold rings in his ears). And the ambassador kept sending letters home to his own government, telling the news.

After a while each prince had a dozen ambassadors living in different foreign capitals, all writing letters. The princes began to be much better informed about one another than rulers had ever been before.

And the ambassadors could prepare treaties. Often a prince wrote to his ambassador in a certain foreign state telling him, "We want you to arrange a treaty allowing us to send iron and copper in wagons through that state." Or the letter would say, "You will make every effort to persuade that state to agree to make the following military preparations, which will assist us in the war we plan to fight next year."

After reading one of these letters, the ambassador would get ready to go and talk with the prime minister of the foreign state where he was, or with some of the leading businessmen, perhaps with the ruling prince himself.

In order to try to make these people take him seriously, the ambassador would dress in his finest embroidered velvet doublet and cape. He would wear expensive jewels and have his hair specially waved, oiled, and perfumed. He would practice in front of a mirror how to smile, how to bow to the ladies. If he was clever he might become very skillful in telling useful lies and in bribing some men, bullying others.

The ambassador would try to arrange what his boss wanted. Then he would write home a report of what he had accomplished so far, and ask for further instructions.

This was much more efficient than the old way of sending merely a messenger once every few years with a flag of truce.

At first some kings refused to allow a bunch of foreign ambassadors to hang around. The fellows might be spies (usually were).

But diplomacy was useful. It produced results. More and more treaties began to be written—mostly alliances for war.

Businessmen also liked the new system. The Florentine ambassador bargained for business privileges for Florentines in Rome—in return for similar privileges granted to Roman merchants in Florence. After these talks a convoy of twenty carts full of copper could pass safely from one state to another. Its price and the rules for selling it had all been arranged by the ambassadors. Its fate was no longer left to chance. More wagons and more ships full of merchandise began to go back and forth among the countries.

Between 1500 and 1648 the kings in Europe one by one decided to send and receive ambassadors.

At the Peace of Westphalia in 1648, ending the Thirty Years' War, they all for the first time accepted the new system.

Nowadays our ambassadors don't put perfume in their hair. But they still practice in front of mirrors, and they still do plenty of bribing and bullying. For this system—diplomacy—is still used. Although it is not very good, it is a lot better than the ancient way, which was no system at all.

After the year 1500 men began to use pistols.

Cannons became larger and stronger. It took ten horses to move one. They were so good that from a distance of half a mile they could bang away at a castle and break off a few stones with every shot. Between shots the men had to wait and let the big gun cool. But within a week one cannon could tear a great gap in the wall, even if it was twenty feet thick. Castles became useless, and people stopped building them.

Most of the soldiers still fought with pikes. (A pike was a long wooden pole with a blade like a fancy butcher

knife on the end of it.) But someone invented the mus-
ket, which was lighter and easier to aim than the big old
harquebus. Then the new armies consisted of cavalry-
men, pikemen, and musketeers. These men shared the
job of shooting the cannons.

The worst slaughter that had been seen up to that
time was the Thirty Years' War. From 1618 to 1648
Catholics and Protestants all over Germany killed one
another vigorously for the love of Jesus Christ. French,
Spanish, Austrian, Swedish, and English soldiers pitched
in from time to time to help.

Gustavus Adolphus, king of Sweden, invented a useful light cannon. It could be pulled rapidly by two
horses, yet it was strong enough to kill many men. In
the Thirty Years' War he would maneuver three dozen
of these gadgets on the two flanks of a battlefield. He
made lots of work for the gravediggers.

The soldiers burned the standing wheat and the barns
and the peasants' hovels. Famines and epidemic diseases killed as efficiently as the best soldiers. At the end
of the thirty years the population of Germany had been
reduced by one-third.

During the fighting a quiet little monk in Paris,
named Emeric Crucé, wrote a small book. It was called
The New Cyneas and was published in 1623. Cyneas
had been an ancient Greek who gave advice to kings.
This book was full of new advice to kings.

The little monk saw that diplomacy was not enough. It did not stop wars. Countries needed some better way to meet and talk, to do business with each other, and to settle their disagreements.

Emeric Crucé's plan was like those of Pierre Dubois, George Podiebrad, and Erasmus. But times had changed. Men's minds had been opened. The new plan was much larger.

This little monk wanted ambassadors from all the nations in the world (including India and China) to meet continuously in Venice. Every important dispute between countries anywhere should be brought to this Council of Ambassadors. They would hear both sides in the dispute. The ambassadors would discuss it and settle it by majority vote.

They would make laws for the world. They would set up a world police force. If any princes disobeyed, the council would "appease them by gentle means, if possible—or, if necessary, by force."

He did not know that 327 years later his idea would be used by the United Nations in Korea.

More and more plans like that were written.

The Duc de Sully's *Memoirs*, published in 1662, contained a project that became especially famous. He claimed that King Henry IV of France had thought it up. Years later Benjamin Franklin wrote to a friend in Paris, "I do not see why you may not in Europe carry the project of good Henry the 4th into execution by form-

ing a federal union of all its different states and kingdoms."

William Penn in 1694 wrote an *Essay Towards the
Present and Future Peace of Europe.* And several other
books of peace plans were written during that century.

The plans were much alike. A congress of ambassadors would settle any dispute between nations. If a nation refused to obey a decision of this congress, all the
other nations must send soldiers to attack the trouble-
making country.

Gradually these plans were becoming better, more
practical. Each writer learned from the books that had
been written before.

The work of William Penn and those other peace-
makers must have been discouraging. They wrote plans
which nobody used. Much of the best work in this world
has seemed very discouraging at the time when it was
done. Those men had no way of knowing that actually
they were little by little preparing the League of Nations and our United Nations.

One writer had more influence than all the others
in that century. He was Hugo Grotius, a Dutch lawyer.

In 1619 in a conflict between two Protestant sects he
was sentenced to life imprisonment for his religious be-
liefs and was locked in a prison at Louvestein, just south
of Utrecht, in Holland. There he was allowed to receive
books in a large chest. Sometimes his laundry and the

volumes he had read were packed in the chest and carried away.

At first the prison guards carefully searched the chest each time, but his wife noticed that after two years they became careless about this. Then she persuaded him to curl up in the chest, and she covered him with some dirty clothes.

The two soldiers who carried it out complained.

One said, "It's awful heavy."

The other added, joking, "There must be a Methodist in it."

Grotius' wife answered, "There are indeed Methodist books in it."

The chest rode on a canal barge to Gorcum (now called Gorinchem), where the bargemen wanted to put it on a bumpy sled. But the maid of Grotius' wife told them, "There are breakable things in it."

Finally it was strapped on a horse and carried slowly to the house of a friend of Grotius, where it was opened. There he disguised himself as a bricklayer. Carrying a hod on his shoulder and a trowel in his hand, he escaped into France.

Four years later, in 1625, his book was published: *The Laws of War and Peace*.

Without trying to invent very much, he had gathered together and put in order all the best of international law that had ever actually been used up to that time.

Many kings and prime ministers read his book and

were startled by the idea that there was any such thing as international law. Couldn't a sovereign do whatever he liked? What international law could any king have to obey?

That book pointed out that in this world no one— not even a king—can be entirely free to do as he pleases.

If the French king wanted the French ambassador to be treated well in Madrid, the French king had to respect the Spanish ambassador in Paris whether he liked him or not. This fact had grown up by custom till it was as good as law.

Also, when two or three kings made a treaty together, they had to obey it. If they promised, for instance, to allow one another's couriers to carry letters back and forth, they must do it.

That is what *international law* means. It means that nations and kings are not entirely free. They must at least obey their own treaties. And they ought to obey certain customs.

Inspired by these new ideas, the makers of peace plans set to work again. War continued to become worse. Better cannons and muskets were invented, and armies grew larger. And scholars soon saw why even international law could not stop war.

If you shoot a man and steal his automobile, the police of your state or nation may catch you. Then a judge and jury will try you, and an officer of the law will put a cold iron bracelet on your wrist and lead you to jail. The police, the courts, and the jails are agencies to enforce the law.

But there were no world police or courts or jails to enforce the treaties and customs that were called international law. So it was not strong enough to stop war.

Charles de Saint-Pierre, a French clergyman (who was called an abbé) studied law and became an adviser to noblemen and politicians. While he was secretary to the French ambassador in the Netherlands in 1713 he dug up the old peace plan of King Henry IV and improved it and rewrote it and republished it.

The famous philosopher Jean Jacques Rousseau edited Saint-Pierre's plan and improved it and rewrote it and published his version in 1761.

There were a great many differences of detail in these and other peace plans written at that time, but the main things they asked for were the same.

Every nation would send delegates to a city in Switzerland. This congress of delegates of all the nations would meet continuously. They would make laws—world laws that could be enforced. They would appoint the judges of an international court.

Any two nations that had a quarrel must send lawyers and witnesses to this court. The judges would decide who was in the wrong and what should be done about it.

If the governing officials of any country were to disobey the court or break the world laws or prepare for war, all the other nations must send their soldiers to restore law and order in that country. The king, prince, prime minister, and generals of the lawbreaking country would then be tried and be either hanged or sent to jail.

This was a brave plan. It would enforce world law and stop wars entirely. Many people were in favor of it.

Let's imagine that it was actually tried. Then we shall see whether it could have worked.

Suppose the congress did meet in Switzerland. And suppose a war broke out again between England and Ireland. (They often did fight.)

The Irish would put seven lawyers and twenty witnesses on a sailboat, which might be delayed by storms and reach the Netherlands after two or three weeks. They would then go on horseback to Switzerland in another week.

When they arrived at the world capital, all the congressmen and judges might be on hand and would take action immediately. (Or there might be some delay getting them together.) The English delegates would be asked for their side of the story. They would ask for time in which to get instructions from their government.

They would write letters. By horseback three couriers wearing handsome leather gloves and with fine plumes in their hats would set out northward, carrying the letters. After an eight- or nine-day ride on muddy roads they would reach Calais. They would go out on the water in a wooden boat with beautiful white sails, and hope the wind would blow.

In London they would have to wait, because the king's investigators must go by horseback and sailboat to the battlefields in Ireland to find out what really was happening there. These investigators might return to London in three weeks. Then the English lawyers and witnesses would prepare their side of the case and set out for Switzerland. Another journey of ten days or two weeks.

How much time would have passed since the first battle!

Then the congress or the world court could discuss the war for a few days and make a decision. Finally they would send their own couriers to London and to Dublin—another two weeks' journey—to tell what had been decided.

Before these final messages arrived, the war could have been fought and ended, with one side defeated entirely.

And how could the same world organization have handled a dispute in Australia or China? It took a sailboat six months to go out there and another six months to come back.

Those days were not like ours. Now if men begin to slaughter each other by thousands somewhere in Asia, the news goes instantly to New York by radio. In twenty-four hours the United Nations Security Council can meet. If the delegates vote, calling all nations to help to stop the aggression, airplanes can take off and be at the fighting front in a few hours.

Back in 1761 Rousseau wrote his plan for a world congress—depending on horses and sailboats. He himself said he did not believe it would work.

5. *America Shows How*

FAR AWAY across the Atlantic Ocean hundreds of French and English soldiers were killing one another in the leafy forests of North America. Indians joined one side or the other and burned the homes of American farmers.

In 1754 seven colonies—from New Hampshire to Maryland—sent delegates to try to make peace with the Iroquois League of Six Nations. Benjamin Franklin, a successful Philadelphia printer, was one of the gentlemen who rode on horseback in the sweet-smelling green

41

springtime along the forest paths. All carried guns, as they expected an attack by a French army.

The little village of Albany was more than a century old. In the public square, among the old houses, the gentlemen in silk coats talked with the red-skinned Iroquois leaders of the League of Six Nations. Would they make peace? The gentlemen offered certain advantages in trade. They made promises.

But the Indians shrugged their shoulders. They were a strong union. The colonies were separate and weak. The Indians refused to make peace.

The gentlemen became angry and discouraged.

Next morning in the red brick meeting hall Mr. Franklin spoke. In one hand he held a pamphlet written and printed by himself. It was a plan—another peace plan. He had got the idea by reading of the Achaean League and of King Henry IV.

He asked, "Is it not plain good sense that all the British provinces in America should join together like members of one family?" The elected assembly of each colony, he suggested, ought to choose delegates and send them to Philadelphia to form an American congress. It would make laws for the whole union of colonies, from New Hampshire to Georgia. And they would ask the king of England to appoint one governor for North America.

The gentlemen at Albany discussed Franklin's plan. It would make the colonies stronger. It would make the

Iroquois League respect them. It would make them strong enough to defeat the French.

These representatives of seven colonies voted for Franklin's *Plan of Union*. They sent printed copies hopefully to the assemblies of all the colonies.

But the colonial assemblies rejected it, because it would have taken some power away from them.

The king of England and his advisers in London also read the plan. They rejected it, because it would have made the colonies too strong.

That was how the United States of America began. One man read history, then wrote a plan. Others talked about it. Some liked it. But it was a failure.

Our world organization, the United Nations, began the same way. During six centuries men wrote plans which were failures. But men kept on trying.

In America the second attempt also was a failure.

September 5, 1774, delegates from twelve colonies met at Philadelphia. Most of these gentlemen had been chosen by revolutionary committees or elected at mass meetings. They gathered to discuss how the colonies could resist the British government. How many soldiers could they find? Who would pay for guns?

The British army and navy had forbidden any ships to enter Boston Harbor until Massachusetts would pay for the cargoes of tea that had been dumped overboard in the Boston Tea Party. A large sum of money was demanded by the tyrant king who gave the colonists no rights. They would rather fight than pay it.

Benjamin Franklin again spoke to the gentlemen in knee breeches and white silk stockings. These colonies, he said, ought to join together in a league. He read his second plan.

They should choose delegates for a congress every year. This congress would make war and accept treaties of peace. It would elect both a president and a general for the army (as the Achaean League had done). It would regulate commerce and make one kind of money for all the states. In case of a quarrel between two states, the congress would hear both sides of the dispute, discuss it, and settle it. (This plan was almost exactly the same as the ancient Achaean League.)

But just then each colony seemed to have only one subject it wanted to argue about: whether or not to make itself independent of England. They did not want to give up any of that brand new sovereign independence, which they had not yet even got. So they rejected Franklin's plan.

But the shot that was heard round the world was fired a few months later, April 19, 1775.

The outbreak of war taught some of the leaders in the thirteen states that they must hang together or they would hang separately. June 7, 1776, another congress at last voted that the states should join together in a league or confederation of some sort.

A month later, July 4, they voted for the Declaration of Independence, proudly calling themselves "The United States of America."

They were not united at all. This was only talk.

But it was brave talk, and it was followed slowly by action. Any big organization, like the United States government or the United Nations, could not come into existence all at once. It had to grow.

That congress of ambassadors appointed a committee of thirteen—one man from each state—to write a plan for a league.

The committee met, talked, argued. The idea still seemed very new, very frightening. At first they could scarcely agree on any part of it. They worked for more than a year.

In June, 1775, the congress of ambassadors had chosen George Washington to lead an army. What army? They asked the states please to send soldiers.

Some states did; others did not. Washington gathered a small army and began to fight the British systematically. The long, slow War for American Independence ground along in blood and suffering.

The Americans had no gunpowder, because the British had forbidden them to manufacture anything. Gentlemen farmers, who had studied science as a hobby, read books on chemistry, hired some workers, and began to produce gunpowder.

A few of the backwoodsmen had handmade flintlock rifles. These had been invented long before but had been considered too hard to make. Only a few existed. But they shot much straighter than the smooth-barrel muskets. The Americans set to work, built factories, invented machines, made rifles.

After a year's work the Articles of Confederation were completed. If Americans could build guns, they could also build a plan of government. Messengers galloped off on horseback, carrying printed copies to all the state legislatures.

Although it was not a strong plan, the men who had written it were still a little afraid of it. So they made one important mistake. They decided that the confederation would not begin unless all the states accepted it— all.

Within one year twelve states did accept it. But not Maryland. So the confederation could not begin to work.

Instead, the thirteen separate states continued to send ambassadors informally to meet at Philadelphia. They called themselves the Continental Congress.

This congress pleaded with the states to send more soldiers, more food, more clothing, more money to pay for the expensive new rifles and gunpowder. The states sent less than half the money needed. Often the soldiers were without pay, often hungry, ragged.

But with French help they won the war.

After the fighting had ended, Maryland accepted the plan. At last, in 1781, the confederation began.

The plan was like the United Nations. It was called "the United States."

For the next eight years this is how it worked:

Each state sent any number up to seven delegates to the congress in New York. But each state had only one vote. (In the U.N. General Assembly in New York each nation has up to five delegates—plus five alternates— and only one vote.) All important questions were decided by two-thirds majority (as in the U.N.). The delegates were not elected by the people; they were appointed by the governor or the legislature of each state (as U.N. delegates are).

There was no president. (The U.N. has none either.) There were no national courts. (The U.N. does have a World Court, but with no power—no jails, for instance.)

The confederation did not act directly on the people. The citizens did not vote for it. It could not tax anyone. It could not arrest anyone. (The U.N. is exactly the same.)

In case of a quarrel between two states, the congress

could act as a court to settle the trouble (just as the U.N. does).

The United Nations is so much like the confederation that we wonder whether the United Nations will soon go through the same change that the confederation did at the end of its eight years.

For the confederation could not last long. It had to change.

While it lasted, all the states continued to have different kinds of money (as the nations do in the United Nations). New Jersey, where many battles had been fought and towns burned, had been so badly damaged by the war that the people were very poor. The state printed paper money to keep them going. But New York city and Philadelphia refused to accept this money. So the New Jersey money lost its value, and the people were in worse condition than before.

New Jersey farmers were selling a great deal of food—mostly vegetables, pigs, and chickens—to New York. New York collected a tax (a tariff) on all this food and also on firewood from Connecticut. A tariff always comes out of the pockets of the people selling the things. So the farmers of New Jersey and Connecticut became angry.

When ships sailed into New York Harbor loaded with cloth, furniture, and tools from Europe, some of these things were going to New Jersey and to Connecticut. But New York collected a tax on them all and would not share the money with New Jersey or Connecticut, who needed it.

New Jersey became angry about this and replied by laying a tremendous, ridiculous tax on a lighthouse at Sandy Hook, which had been leased to New York. New York needed the lighthouse. Connecticut farmers formed a farmers' union to refuse to sell anything to New York. Congress could not settle the dispute, because it was not strong enough to make New York give up any of its tax money.

Congress, having no power itself to tax anybody, ran badly into debt. The superintendent of finances of the so-called United States resigned. He said no honest man could go on borrowing money for the confederation, which was too weak even to pay interest.

After six years of this mess twelve states chose delegates to meet as a special convention and try to improve the Articles of Confederation.

They got together in Independence Hall in Philadelphia. Benjamin Franklin was the oldest man present. George Washington, former Commander-in-Chief of the Continental Army, was elected president of the convention. Alexander Hamilton, James Madison, and several other men now famous in history were among the delegates.

They worked all summer, four months. It was the hottest summer that had been felt in almost forty years.

Of the fifty-five delegates appointed, usually about thirty were at the meetings. They came and went. Alexander Hamilton wanted a strong government with a king at the head of it. At first most of the other delegates would not even consent to one with a President. Disgusted, Hamilton went home to New York. George Washington wrote to him, asking him to come back, and he did.

The delegates discussed several plans, made many compromises. During those four months a constitution slowly grew. Every part of the proposed new government was developed little by little, each man contributing some ideas. What one man said made another think of something.

By September they had designed a government which no one of them could have invented alone. There would be a President, national courts and jails, a congress with power to make laws and levy taxes. Every state would be equal in the Senate by having two Senators. But in the House each state would have a different number of representatives according to the size of its population.

On September 17, 1787, George Washington called the delegates to order for the last time. The new Constitution of the United States, neatly copied out on parchment, lay on a table. Most of the gentlemen signed it. (Two were afraid to.)

But it was not in force yet. Near the end it said that it

would take effect as soon as nine of the states accepted it. Not all thirteen this time; only nine.

The voters of each state had to elect delegates to a special state convention, which would accept or reject the Constitution.

Immediately the hottest debate began. Men became candidates for these conventions and made electioneering speeches, some for the Constitution, some against it. Voters talked back at them in public meetings. A flood of talk swept over the country.

Some cried out that if the people accepted the Constitution they would lose all their liberties. Some warned that if nine states set up the new government, they would immediately be at war with the other four.

But some said, "The Constitution offers the thirteen states their only hope for safety, self-respect, and prosperity."

Washington pointed out in a letter to a friend, "It is a novel and astonishing spectacle to see a whole people deliberating calmly on what form of government they will have—instead of deciding it by war or revolution."

One by one a few states accepted it. New Hampshire rejected it, then voted again in June, 1788, and accepted it. The United States Constitution was in force. Four days later Virginia followed.

New York, not wanting to be left out, ratified in time

to take part in the first election. Eleven states chose George Washington to be President.

He was inaugurated April 30, 1789, while the new Senate and House of Representatives met and began to make rules for themselves.

For the next seven months, till it ratified, North Carolina was treated as a foreign nation.

In 1790 the new Senate passed a bill saying no one in the United States could buy anything from or sell anything to anybody in the other foreign country, Rhode Island. This was a threat.

At last, more than a year after Washington's inauguration, a convention met in Rhode Island and by a small majority voted to join the United States.

It was the first federal union in modern times. There had been old ones—the Achaean League, for example—but never before had there been such a large one.

It was followed by others: Switzerland became a federal union, Canada, Argentina, Mexico, and many more. The method works.

Benjamin Franklin wrote to a friend in Paris that the same type of union should be created in Europe. Now, 165 years later, that is beginning to be done.

Could one government like this be made for the whole world?

6. *Human Rights*

WAR WAS growing. Cannons became stronger and better designed. They could shoot farther and could aim better.

The French Revolution ended with Napoleon's becoming dictator. He was a military genius. He invented more effective ways to use cannons. For the first time the big guns in his army were fired by specially trained artillery experts. They could kill, wound, tear apart thousands of men in a few minutes.

He also trained enormous numbers of foot soldiers and cavalry, armed with flintlock rifles.

With these forces he conquered Germany, conquered Austria, conquered Italy, conquered Spain. He marched a colossal French army all the way to Moscow. But he lost it on the snow-covered steppes. The Frenchmen who were not shot were frozen to death in the Russian winter.

Flintlocks were replaced by percussion caps in 1842. Breech-loading rifles came into use in 1852. Machine guns in 1860.

These weapons were marvelously effective. War casualties were no longer counted in thousands but in hundreds of thousands. And armies grew larger and larger. They became more and more expensive. Higher taxes had to be collected. Each nation spent a larger part of its money, manpower, and time on war and preparations for war.

Why did wars begin? There have been four main causes.

1. Wars have been caused partly by politics. Government leaders have used war as an excuse to make their people obedient. The Korean war was useful to Mao Tse-tung, the Communist dictator of China. Chinese who would have resisted him in time of peace gave up resisting because they wanted to be loyal to their country in time of war.

But the leaders can be prevented from doing this. In a democracy the voters can stop them.

2. Wars have been caused partly by human feelings, emotions, excitement. Alexander the Great and Genghis Khan started wars because they yearned to conquer, to have more power, to rule over more people. Napoleon and Hitler both became furious, lost their heads, and attacked Russia. Patriots sometimes yell for war to defend their nation's honor or to win glory.

In a democracy these mistakes can be prevented. If the President becomes too excited, Congress can control him. If a few Congressmen go berserk, the others can vote against them.

3. Wars have been caused partly by money, business, trade. If two nations want the same oil wells, they may fight. It has been said that World War I started because Germany had taken away too much of England's overseas trade and wanted even more.

But England and Germany are still competing. Two wars did not solve the problem. Wars never do. It can be worked out only by sensible talk, by sharing the markets, by letting each country have a fair part of the airlines and other businesses.

The nations will all be richer if the U.N. can make them talk and work together instead of fighting.

4. Some wars have been caused partly by a clash between two systems of belief, two isms. Christianity against Mohammedanism in the Crusades. Then Prot-

estant Christianity against Catholic Christianity in the Thirty Years' War. In World War II it was Fascist militarism against democracy and communism. Must we have another, of democracy against communism?

This cause of war can be prevented. A strong United Nations could stand guard between any two systems. It should not let one threaten the other.

Those have been the four main causes of wars: politics, emotions, money, and ideas. No one of them has ever been the sole cause of a war. Usually three, sometimes all four started the slaughter.

And all four can be peacefully controlled.

A great step forward toward controlling them was made in the first years of the French Revolution. Something new and important came into the making of peace plans.

In France before the Revolution if a man dared to write the truth about what the government officials were doing, and if they did not like what he wrote, they secretly locked him in jail. He had no trial, no chance to defend himself before a jury.

Taxes were too high. Many people were starving, and the government did nothing to help them. Too many government officials were cheating, stealing, or granting privileges to any criminal who would pay them a bribe.

Could newspapers try to protect the people by printing the truth about this? Some pamphlets about it were distributed secretly. If the authors were caught, they were tortured. Even Voltaire, though he was a nobleman, was locked up for a while in the old prison called the Bastille because his pen was too bold in defense of the people.

In Paris on a wild night of shouting, singing, and cannon fire (two and a half months after Washington's inauguration) a mob attacked the Bastille. They killed the king's guardsmen and began to tear down the building entirely. The prisoners, most of whom had been locked up only because the king disliked them, were set free. The French Revolution began.

The French National Assembly that summer, 1789, passed a Declaration of the Rights of Man. It promised to all citizens freedom of speech, freedom of religion, freedom from being put in prison except when they broke some law.

In America the United States Congress passed the first ten amendments to the Constitution. These amendments were quickly accepted by the states. They are called a Bill of Rights because they promise to all citizens freedom of speech, freedom of religion, freedom from illegal imprisonment.

In Paris an extraordinary man got himself elected into the National Assembly. He was a wealthy Prussian, Jean Baptiste du Val de Grâce, Baron von Cloots, known as the Orator of the Human Race. He gave an enormous sum of money to the new French Republic.

In 1792 in a fiery speech that made the National Assembly cheer and shout, he presented his plan to keep world peace. He called it *The Universal Republic.*

His plan was like the Constitution of the United States. He said the whole world should have one government. Voters everywhere would elect delegates to a world parliament. It would make world laws, abolish armies, set up a world police to protect people, and create one kind of money.

In each country or district the people could speak their own language, have their own books, newspapers, schools, churches. Most important of all, the world government would have a Bill of Rights, promising to all people everywhere freedom of speech, freedom of religion, freedom from being put in jail except when they had committed some crime.

The delegates in the French National Assembly cheered.

But then they looked at one another and shrugged. How could they create a universal republic? By conquering the whole world? No, thank you.

However, something new had been introduced into the making of peace plans: human rights. Freedom for the whole world.

It began with one man talking. Others liked the idea. Naturally the first attempt was a failure. Big, important things always begin that way.

And people kept on talking about freedoms for every-one. A hundred and fifty-five years later the United Nations voted a Declaration of Human Rights for the whole world. The idea is growing stronger. What will it do next?

Immanuel Kant, the famous German philosopher, wrote in 1795 a plan for a league of nations. Jeremy Bentham, the English philosopher, wrote another around 1790, which was published fifty years later. In 1840 William Ladd in the United States wrote one, too, which was much talked about in the Peace Societies founded by him.

These plans were more cautious than von Cloots's *The Universal Republic.* They said merely that delegates from all nations should meet together in an international assembly. It should recommend ways in which the nations could get along with each other peacefully. It should appoint judges to an international court.

These plans sound like the real League of Nations, which began a century later. The idea had already been growing for five centuries, ever since Pierre Dubois' book in 1306. But the world was still not ready for even this cautious plan.

First the nations had to try the simplest possible form of the idea: working together at all. They had never done even that.

The first experiment in working together was crude, brutal.

After Napoleon's defeat at Waterloo in 1815 the kings of Russia, Prussia, and Austria had some long talks together. They were afraid of the ideas of liberty that had been stirred up by the French Revolution.

So they joined together in what they called the Holy Alliance (for an unholy purpose). They agreed that if democracy again arose in any country they would send in their armies and suppress it.

For a while they were successful. They sent their armies into Spain and into two states in Italy (Naples and Piedmont).

The Holy Alliance was soon joined by France. England was sometimes in, sometimes out. Within six years they met in five big official conferences.

In 1823 they were feeling cocky and decided to suppress some of the new democratic governments in South America.

When this news reached the United States, President Monroe spoke to Congress. If any foreign armies, he said, tried to march into any country anywhere in the Americas, the United States would go to war to defend these continents. That was the Monroe Doctrine.

The United States Navy polished its guns. And the Europeans had to leave South America alone.

Revolutions all over Europe in 1830 and 1848 put an end to the Holy Alliance. Democracy was winning.

However, while it lasted, the Holy Alliance had made a tremendous achievement. It had shown that nations could work together.

Soon afterwards—in 1856—the nations tried a second experiment in working together.

They sent delegates to a conference in Paris. These gentlemen discussed the Danube River. Lots of shoes, kitchen stoves, wine, vegetables, pigs, and coal were being sent up and down the river in barges. And the businessmen had plenty of trouble. The river passed through or by several countries, all of which collected taxes on every barge and made different rules.

The delegates at Paris did more than talk about this problem. They planned an international organization called the Danube Commission.

Soon afterward it was accepted by the governments of the countries that did business on the river. It began to work.

The commission consisted of men appointed by those governments. It made all the rules for the whole river. Taxes were abolished. Instead the commission collected dues of its own. With this money it built bridges, dikes, towpaths. It hired soldiers to police the river. It appointed judges, set up its own courts. It could arrest a barge owner who broke its rules, try him, and fine him if he was guilty.

And the countries along the river actually let it do

all this. They gave up their right to make rules for the river. They gave up their right to tax goods carried on the river. They gave up part of their sovereignty (a very small part, obviously).

The commission was successful. It lasted ninety-two years.

In 1775 scarcely anyone in Europe would have believed that such an international organization was possible. Weren't nations independent, sovereign? Couldn't a nation do as it pleased? Then how could nations create an international commission that had real power, and give up to it some of their right to do as they pleased?

Well, they tried, and they succeeded. People were learning.

And that commission was only a beginning.

7. *International Unions*

In 1832 a lively middle-aged man with a bushy beard, Samuel Morse, was returning to America. Although he was already a well-known artist, founder and president of the American Academy of Design, he had just spent three years in Europe, studying old-master paintings.

On board a steamship called the *Sully* he and some of the other passengers talked about recent discoveries about electricity. It could make a rod of iron become a magnet. And the iron would stop being a magnet the moment the electricity stopped.

Morse was able to understand this because he had once studied electricity at Yale. But electricity was mysterious. Very little had been known about it. The new discoveries excited his artist's imagination. He told the other passengers that electromagnets could be used for sending messages.

He began to sketch pictures. Some of his portraits were so good that they are still shown in museums. But at that moment he was not making a portrait. He sketched imaginary gadgets—little telegraph machines. Within two days he had invented one that looked as though it would work. The captain of the ship urged him to build it.

Back in the United States, Morse tried. But, being an artist, he did not have much money. In a little shop in New Haven he worked hard for four years. He slept on a cot in the shop, cooked his own meals, often went hungry. But he built telegraph machines. He invented the Morse code.

At last he got a batch of copper wire. In 1837 in a demonstration for a few professors at the University of the City of New York he sent messages through long coils of wire wound round a lecture room.

After another seven years, in 1844, the United States Congress granted him enough money to build a telegraph line from Washington to Baltimore.

Several inventors in England, France, and Germany were designing telegraph gadgets, too, though Morse's were the first and the most useful. Wires began to be strung up connecting many cities. In 1851 a cable was laid under the English Channel, completing the line from London to Paris.

This was the invention for which Pierre Dubois, Emeric Crucé, von Cloots, and the other writers of world-peace plans had been wishing. At last messages could be sent instantly over great distances. For the first time world organization began to be possible.

Another conference of delegates from many nations met in Paris in 1864. This time the dignified gentlemen in dark business suits and beards of many shapes came to discuss this new problem: telegrams.

More and more people were telegraphing their urgent messages. All over Europe the wires crossed national boundaries.

But each country charged different prices and had different rules. Telegrams often did not arrive.

The delegates of twenty nations, meeting at Paris, wrote a plan for an International Telegraphic Union. Copies of the plan were sent to all the capitals. One by one the governments accepted it.

In 1865 the union began. It moved into a building in Berne, Switzerland, and hired a number of engineers, accountants, bankers, clerks, office boys.

The nations that belonged to it gave it a little money. Every few years they sent delegates again to meet and decide what the union would do. And the office at Berne worked all the time.

It gathered information about telegraph rates and regulations in all countries. It helped the nations to agree on one scale of prices and one set of rules. After that anybody could much more easily send a telegram from his country to someone in a foreign country.

As years passed, more nations joined. The union's work was enlarged to include trans-Atlantic cables.

Later it was enlarged again to include telephones and radio. Then the name was changed to the International Telecommunication Union. It began to hold international conferences about radio wave-lengths.

It is still working successfully. The United States is a member. Eighty-one countries are members. Now it includes television. And it has become connected to the United Nations.

Naturally that first international union was for communication. Always the great problem between nations had been: How could they talk to each other?

The second union was for communication, too. It was for mail and post offices.

It was much needed. Faster ships were being invented. More factories were being built, making kitchen stoves, oil lamps, cotton cloth, guns, and thousands of other things. Consequently more business was being done. Therefore the quantity of letters, advertisements, and bills being mailed—many of them across national boundaries—was increasing enormously.

Mail to another country was expensive. And all countries charged different prices. Often letters were delayed for many weeks by the different regulations, or did not arrive at all.

During the Civil War the United States postmaster general, Montgomery Blair, called a conference of postal officials. Coming from fifteen nations, they met in Paris in May, 1863. They discussed plans for an international postal organization of some sort.

At first they could not agree. Each plan they thought of only caused an argument. Making an international organization was still a fairly new experience. The politicians were not at all sure that it would work. And they did not trust one another.

But more nations joined the discussions. During eleven years of talking and arguing in several international conferences, at last a good plan was made.

In 1874 twenty-two nations together set up the General Postal Union with an office at Berne. In the next four years so many more joined that they proudly changed the name to the Universal Postal Union.

It has been working ever since. Every nation in the world is now a member (eight-six countries). It has become connected to the United Nations.

Now when you want to send a letter to someone in a faraway country, you can put on a five-cent stamp, slip your letter into a mailbox, and feel confident. Men and women wearing the postal uniforms of several different nations may handle your letter. What is this union which makes it possible for them to work together?

The union has two parts: a conference and an office staff.

The nations send delegates to a conference every five years or more. Sometimes the conferees have to wait till a war is ended. Sometimes they don't wait; they meet anyway. This is one place where enemies sit down together and do business. During World War II, German Nazis, Russian Communists, and American democrats worked together round a table at Berne.

Between conferences the office of the union goes on working, in peace and in war. The office consists of a director, a vice-director, and a whole building full of secretaries.

When a letter is mailed in Afghanistan addressed to someone in Canada, the Universal Postal Union has already decided whose railroads and whose ships will carry it. A letter may pass through five or six countries. Who pays all those countries for taking care of it?

The Postal Union has an easy system. It keeps records. And once a year the clerks in the office figure out how much money each country owes to every other country for mail carried that year. Usually we owe Mexico and

Siam about the same amount that they owe us, maybe a little more. The balance that we pay is very small.

At last a new method had been created by which nations could work together. It was a long forward step.

First came the messenger in ancient times carrying a flag of truce and accompanied ·by two horn-blowing heralds. Then the ambassador in the sixteenth century, living at a foreign capital and practicing his smiles before a mirror. And then the international organization, its office connected by telegraph wires to every nation in the world.

How does it work?

Each of these unions has two parts: a conference and an office staff. The conference consists of delegates from all the member nations. Usually each nation has one vote. The delegates meet every year or once in three years or once in five years. They decide what the union shall do.

Then the staff does it. The staff consists of men and women employed by the union. They become experts. They have offices in a building and work there all year long.

Because the method was good, it began to grow. The Postal Union was soon followed by others.

Two years later came the International Bureau of Weights and Measures. The United States joined. This bureau still exists. Thirty-three nations are members.

International unions were formed for the protection of patents and trademarks and of copyrights for books.

The International Union of Railway Freight Transportation helped straighten out prices and rules. It found a solution to the big problem of freight cars.

A freight car may carry cans of olive oil from Spain to Poland. It is then filled with wheat and sent to Belgium. Loaded with cheeses, it goes back into Germany. It takes lumber into Italy and ends up empty on a sidetrack somewhere. Where? How can the owner find it and bring it home again?

He consults the international organization. They have a system.

The invention of the telegraph made international organization possible. Consequently nations began to have new responsibilities.

How must a country act if it joins such an organization? (How must you behave to your friends if you join a club with them?)

In 1902 the International Sugar Commission showed part of the answer.

A number of nations signed an agreement promising to obey the decisions of this international group of experts. It collected facts. It found that certain countries ought to lower their tariffs on sugar. Then those countries had to do it, because they had promised.

That was surprising. Until then most of our politicians had talked as though a sovereign nation could do as it pleased. They shouted that no international group, mostly foreigners, could ever make us lower our tariffs if we didn't want to.

But when our nation joins with other nations, we have to respect the majority. Often they make us lower a tariff or change some law when we don't want to.

Also, we are often part of a majority that makes France or Peru do something they dislike.

That is fair play. When you are a member of a club, you have to accept the decisions of the majority. And that is what nations have to do in order to get along with one another without fighting wars.

An American, David Lubin, traveled all over Europe trying to persuade government officials that farmers needed the help of one of these international organizations.

American farmers sold thousands of tons of wheat every year to countries in Europe and Asia. Insect pests —locusts, for example—traveled from one country to another without stopping at the border to ask permission. Couldn't the nations work together to help farmers get paid for the food they sent abroad? And couldn't the nations warn one another of mass movements of bugs?

At last the Italian government was interested. They called the other nations to a conference.

The International Institute of Agriculture began

work in 1905 with an office in Rome. More and more nations joined. Soon it had seventy-four members.

It was later replaced by the United Nations agency called the Food and Agriculture Organization. In 1951 FAO moved into a new building in Rome called the David Lubin Building.

The International Office of Public Health began in 1907. With its help the government medical officers of many nations tried to work together.

At first they accomplished very little, because their governments were not yet interested in health and would not spend money on it. But the organization made some plans to try to stop cholera, malaria, and other diseases.

The nations also started a great many smaller international organizations.

For example, an international commission operates the lighthouse at Cape Spartel on the coast of Morocco. The United States is a member.

The North Atlantic Ice Patrol is operated by the United States to save ships from icebergs. Other nations contribute money.

In 1914 at least forty-five important international government organizations were at work.

An inventor makes drawings of a machine that he would like to build. Scholars wrote plans for a world organization to keep peace.

Then the inventor builds little models of his machine to see how it will work. The nations created forty-five international organizations, and men began to work them and find out what such things could do.

They were small-scale models for the League of Nations, which came later, and for the United Nations, which came later still.

8. *Four Peaceful Methods*

DIPLOMACY HAS grown a great deal since the first prince
sent an ambassador to live in the capital of a neighboring country. Modern diplomatic service no longer de-
pends on couriers with leather gloves and with feathers
in their hats carrying letters on horseback every week
or two.

In Washington the ambassador from France has a
whole office building full of lawyers, secretaries, research workers, translators, office boys, radio techni-

cians, a cook and cook's assistants, elevator men, janitors, and scrub women.

The United States embassy in Paris occupies a palace and employs seven hundred persons.

In London there are ambassadors from every nation in the world, each in touch with his home government by radio.

What do they do?

The Secretary of State in Washington speaks with the ambassador from Egypt. The Egyptian asks, is Congress willing to lower the tariff on Egyptian rice and cotton if the Egyptians buy certain railway cars from the U.S.A.?

The American shakes his head. No. But would the Egyptian government like to discuss a deal on rice alone?

The Egyptian ambassador excuses himself for half an hour. He telephones to his boss in Cairo 5,850 miles away.

Before lunch he is already back with the answer. They will discuss a deal on rice, provided that date-nut oil is included. The negotiations can continue the same day.

The Swiss ambassador comes hurrying to see the Secretary of State at Washington. The governor of a Swiss canton was murdered an hour ago by an American tourist.

A girl in the State Department building types out an inquiry on a teletype machine. The message is reproduced instantly in the United States embassy in Berne.

Within ten minutes two assistants of our ambassador to Switzerland are in an automobile on their way to the local Swiss police station to talk with the murderer, who claims to be an American.

Is he an American? A few minutes later his photograph is radioed to Washington. Clerks look for him in the records of the passport division.

The whole matter may be settled before the newspapers have even heard of the shooting.

Every day, every week, diplomacy is at work. Claims and complaints are made, discussed, settled.

Every week this method puts a stop to one trouble or another that might otherwise lead to war. If all human beings were intelligent, kind, sweet, and forgiving, could we solve every international dispute by this method?

Well, politicians and businessmen are not angels. Instead they are just as quarrelsome as you and your friends, only they have more to quarrel about. And diplomacy is not enough to settle all those quarrels.

In 1870 France declared war on Prussia. A couple of million men were slaughtered. The Germans surrounded Paris, mounted long-range cannons on a nearby hill, and bombarded the city, killing women and children, too. Diplomacy did not prevent the fighting.

Turkey fought wars with Serbia, Russia, and Greece. England fought Afghanistan and Egypt. China fought

France, then Japan. Wars raged between Serbia and Bulgaria, between Italy and Ethiopia.

Wars were becoming bloodier. Inventors built better machine guns, repeater rifles, submarine torpedoes, cannons that could hit a house ten miles away and kill everyone in it.

Most nations began forcing all their young men to learn how to be soldiers.

All these wars and this military training and these new weapons cost money. Lots of money. More money than had ever before been spent on war. They cost more than the nations could afford.

By 1898 Russia was nearly bankrupt. In most countries many people were hungry because so much money went for war, not for food.

In 1899 Czar Nicholas II of Russia asked all the nations to send delegates to a Peace Conference to try to put a stop to the bloodshed and the expense.

So the First Hague Peace Conference met in The Netherlands. Delegates from twenty-six nations gathered in a large hall (half a dozen or more men from each nation). After a few speeches they divided up into committees and got to work.

One committee wrote a statement recommending good offices and mediation. Soon afterward these were accepted by the governments of most nations.

They meant that if two countries had a quarrel, the president or king of any other country could butt in.

He could send messages to both, asking them to talk it over and stop fighting.

A few years later this was done. Russia and Japan fought a nasty war. So President Theodore Roosevelt sent cablegrams to the czar and the mikado.

Twenty years earlier they would have snorted that it was no business of his. Butting in! The quarrel did not concern him.

But times had changed. The nations had agreed to accept good offices. Why? What right have outsiders to interfere?

Because war anywhere concerns everybody. Modern war is becoming more and more dangerous. It is like fire. Even a small one may spread.

At the First Hague Peace Conference most nations had admitted that this was true.

After much cabling back and forth, the Russians and Japanese still could not settle their differences. They both wanted Port Arthur and the Manchurian Railway. But good offices had not entirely failed. It had opened the way for the next step.

So Roosevelt took the next step. He offered to mediate. He would try to arrange a compromise. Each side would have to give up something. (He did not offer to be a judge.)

Actually the war was going badly for both sides. So they accepted his offer.

Russian and Japanese delegates met at Portsmouth,

New Hampshire. The Americans made suggestions but did not try to say which side was in the wrong.

The result was a peace treaty. Both sides accepted it. The war was ended.

A Russian, Frédéric de Martens, invented another method, called a commission of inquiry. At the First Hague Peace Conference the delegates discussed it and voted for it. It was very soon used.

On the night of October 21, 1904, during the Russian-Japanese War, some British fishing boats were trawling for cod in the North Sea.

Cannons suddenly blazed away at them from Russian warships. Several of the fishing boats were badly damaged. Two Englishmen were killed.

The warships were on their way to the battle zone, looking for Japanese torpedo boats.

When the British people read of this in their newspapers, a great many of them became angry. They shouted that this was the worst of a series of Russian "outrages," and they wouldn't stand for it. While the British ambassador in Petrograd delivered to the Russian minister of foreign affairs a sharply worded cablegram from London, protesting and asking payment of damages, many people in England were demanding war against Russia.

The French butted in. With their help and many cablegrams the two quarreling governments soon agreed to try to settle the fishing-boat problem peacefully.

But they could not agree on the facts. Just what had happened that night?

So both sides signed an agreement, saying that an international commission of inquiry should be appointed. This would consist of five men, all high-ranking naval officers. One would be from Russia, one from England, and three from neutral countries that had nothing to do with the quarrel. The two governments agreed that this commission should decide what really had happened and how much the damage had cost.

The commissioners met in Paris in January, 1905. They heard witnesses. They read documents. In less than two months they announced their findings. They decided that the Russians actually had shot at the fishermen—but only by mistake, thinking they were Japanese—and had caused damage equal to 65,000 pounds in British money.

And then the Russian government paid. The commission of inquiry did not force them to pay. It was only five men whose job was to find out the real facts. But the Russians paid.

This method is still used often. Many quarrels can be settled merely by having some reliable committee find out the real facts.

The First Hague Peace Conference also tried to improve arbitration.

This was an old method. It had been very simple.

As soon as the American Revolutionary War was ended by a peace treaty with England, some of our farmers began to fight with Canadian farmers. The peace treaty said that part of our boundary was the River St. Croix. But two rivers had that name. Which was our boundary?

Both sides tried to collect taxes on the land between the rivers. The two governments sent threatening notes to one another.

The quarrel was settled by arbitration. We chose a man to act as an arbitrator. Canada chose another. These two men together chose a third.

Then the three men met in a courthouse. Lawyers from both sides came and spoke. Official papers—treaties and maps—were handed to the arbitrators. They had to do more than find facts. They had to use their own judgment, because the question was not merely: Which river was called St. Croix? (Both rivers were.) The question was: Which river did the men who wrote the treaty have in mind?

The arbitrators studied the evidence and decided by majority vote. The dispute was ended.

But the method was too simple. It did not always work well.

So the delegates at the First Hague Peace Conference in 1899 wrote rules about how it should be done. And they set up the Permanent Court of Arbitration.

It still exists. And it has recently become important. But it is not a court. It is a list of names of men. Each nation chooses some (not more than four). These men are lawyers or judges or professors who understand international law. Now there are about 150 men on this list.

When two nations have a quarrel, they can choose men from this list to be their arbitrators. Each quarreling nation chooses two, only one of whom can be from that nation. These four together choose a fifth. All must be from the list.

These five men meet somewhere. They hear lawyers and witnesses. Then they decide the case.

In 1922 Norway brought a case against the United States. Norway claimed that during World War I we had illegally seized some ships belonging to Norwegian citizens.

The U.S.A. said, "Shut up. The ships were being built in the United States. They were not even finished. It was wartime. Of course we took them."

But the Norwegians answered, "If you're so sure you're right, why don't you let the question be settled by five arbitrators from the Permanent Court of Arbitration?"

Our State Department agreed.

And the arbitrators decided the U.S.A. had been in the wrong. So the United States Treasury paid the Norwegians twelve million dollars.

In most cases the losing nation accepts the decision of the arbitrators. But not always. In three or four cases they have seemed unfair.

Once they said Venezuela must pay England for some oil, when most people think England had no right to it. Venezuela refused to pay, and never did pay.

All these methods were in use by 1914. Yet they did not prevent World War I.

Diplomacy, good offices and mediation, commission of inquiry, and arbitration were not enough. Something more was needed.

9. *World War I Produced the League*

WHEN TWO schoolboys quarrel over a football, each saying it is his, the schoolteacher or principal can make them submit their dispute to discussion, to a fact-finding investigation, or if necessary to arbitration.

But in 1914, if two nations quarreled over land or trade rights, there was not yet any world organization that could oblige them to submit their dispute to discussion, to a commission of inquiry, or to a committee of arbitrators.

Those methods were not enough because there was no power that could force quarreling nations to use them.

When two men quarrel over a corn field or a vacant lot, each saying it belongs to him, the police and the courts can force them to submit their dispute to a judge and jury. The men are not allowed to shoot it out as nations do.

But in 1914 there were no world police or world courts that could force the leaders of nations to submit their dispute to a fair trial.

In August, 1914, well-trained German armies marched into Belgium and France. Austria, Turkey, and Bulgaria fought on the side of Germany. Russia, Great Britain, and Italy fought against Germany. Others joined, until twenty-nine nations were at war. That is why it was called World War I.

From 1914 to 1918 eight and a half million soldiers were killed. Ten million women, children, farmers and other men not in the fighting were killed by starvation or disease caused by the war. Twenty-two million men were wounded.

The fighting nations spent two hundred billion dollars for their armies. Ships were sunk, railroad trains destroyed by cannon fire. Factories, warehouses, and homes were shot up. The property destroyed was worth a hundred and fifty billion dollars.

For the first time in all the history of the human race one war was so destructive that the entire world for fifteen years mourned and paid for it.

During the continual slaughter for those four years of World War I at least seventeen important books were published asking for a world organization to prevent war.

In 1915 the League to Enforce Peace was formed in America, with an ex-President of the United States— William Howard Taft—at the head of it. In England that year a group of distinguished scholars and politicians began the League of Nations Society. In France and in Germany, too, similar movements got going.

Many people spoke of the peace plans of Pierre Dubois, Emeric Crucé, Baron von Cloots.

While these plans were only talk, world organization in fact had begun in a small way. The Universal Postal Union and the rest of the forty-five international unions were already at work. World organization was too small to stop war yet. But it could grow. Many people were working to make it become more like the plans.

The League to Enforce Peace, the Women's Peace Party, and a dozen other groups in the United States persuaded President Woodrow Wilson to work for a League of Nations.

In November, 1918, as soon as the fighting of World War I ended, large groups of delegates from the victorious nations began to arrive in Paris. President Wilson brought the Secretary of State of the United States, three other high officials, and two hundred college professors, army officers, lawyers, and other experts.

All the Allied nations sent large delegations. Two thousand men worked together for ten months.

The important decisions were made by President Wilson, Premier Clemenceau of France, and Prime Minister Lloyd George of Great Britain. These three gentlemen crawled around on their knees on large maps spread on the floor, redrawing the boundaries of the nations of Europe.

The delegates wrote the treaty of peace, which the Allies were going to force the Germans to sign. They wrote the Covenant of the League of Nations. They also wrote the Constitution of the International Labor Organization.

These three documents were printed together in a pamphlet, which the proud chief delegates of the Allies, together with the angry delegates of defeated Germany, all signed on June 28, 1919. As the actual signing that day was done in a ceremony in the famous palace of Louis XIV at Versailles, the whole pamphlet is called the Treaty of Versailles.

The Germans said that the peace treaty was very severe. Germany had to lose all its colonies in Africa and in the Pacific Ocean. Germany lost pieces of its land, which were handed to Poland, France, Czechoslovakia. And Germany promised to pay enormous sums of money to the Allies as reparations.

By what method could the Allies prevent Germans from seeking revenge twenty years later?

President Wilson had the idea that the League of Nations would prevent this.

When President Wilson went to France for the peace conference, he carried his own typewritten plan for a League of Nations.

At Paris the British and French statesmen met him with similar plans which they had written.

President Wilson stubbornly insisted on his own plan. He allowed the foreign statesmen to change it only in small details. One addition was the new system for taking care of Germany's colonies. This system, called mandates, was invented by General Smuts of South Africa, and President Wilson liked it.

By his powerful oratory Wilson persuaded the delegates of many nations at Paris to accept the complete plan, then entitled the Covenant of the League of Nations.

But when he sailed home he discovered that he had forgotten to consult the Senate of the United States about it.

The Senators saw that if we joined the League we

would have to promise to enforce peace—with guns, if necessary. They made excited speeches, shouting that never again would American boys be sent to lose their lives fighting on foreign soil.

The Senators voted against joining President Wilson's League.

In January, 1920, the League of Nations came into existence. By the end of the year, forty-eight countries had accepted it. As the months passed, others joined, until by 1926 almost the whole world was in it—fifty-five nations. But not the United States.

The League built a large palace at Geneva in Switzerland.

Every year in September the Assembly met. Each member nation could appoint three delegates, but each nation had only one vote.

Most of the delegates wore moustaches and stiff, starched collars. They all had to speak either English or French. After each gentleman said anything in one of these languages, an interpreter repeated it in the other language.

When a time came for a vote, the three delegates from Sweden, for example, whispered together and decided what their one vote would be. Or, if they did not feel sure what their government would want in this case, they would telegraph to Stockholm for instructions.

Important decisions could be made only by unanimous vote. Now we complain that in the United Nations each of the Big Five countries has a veto. But in the League every country had a veto.

Why? Because of the old theory of national sovereignty. A nation was sovereign and could do as it pleased. Or could it? Well, people thought they could. They were not yet ready to accept the idea that a majority should rule.

Of course not. Think what it would mean! Suppose the Assembly discussed a plan for leasing ten ships in which to carry refugees. If the plan was accepted, it would cost money, and every nation must pay a little. And suppose the plan was favored by the votes of fifty-four nations, but Peru was against it.

Could any league or union or world organization of any kind ever oblige Peru to pay its share after it had voted against the plan? Impossible! Think of its national pride! Wasn't that nation sovereign? Couldn't it do as it pleased?

That was the old theory. It had already been disproved by the International Sugar Commission in 1902, but most politicians still clung to it.

The Council of the League was intended to consist of delegates from the Big Five nations and from a few smaller nations. The Big Five were not the same as now. They were the United States, Great Britain, France, Italy, and Japan.

As the United States did not join, the Council became the Big Four, plus a few smaller nations elected by the Assembly.

Each nation that was a member of the Council sent one delegate to it. The Council met for a week or more about every two months.

Every nation that was a member of the Council had a veto. Not only the Big Four. The small ones, too.

The League hired a Secretariat. This consisted of a Secretary-General (Sir Eric Drummond) and a number of translators, scholars, experts on various problems, typists, clerks, librarians. Drummond had the idea of hiring men and women from all over the world. As the work of the League increased, Drummond hired more, till there were 630 workers from thirty-four different countries.

The Council promptly appointed a committee to write a plan for a World Court. The plan was soon accepted. In 1921 the Council and the Assembly together elected the judges.

The League of Nations then consisted of four parts: the Assembly, the Council, the Secretariat, the World Court.

All this cost money. The League could not tax anyone. It could only ask the nations please to give it what it needed. This world organization to keep peace got and spent about six million dollars a year.

That was enough to pay the military expenses of the

United States during World War II for thirty-seven
minutes.

This was the League of Nations.
What did it actually do?

10. *The League Helped People in Trouble*

THE STATESMEN of the various countries stood looking at the League as though it were a new machine. They did not understand it. Was it an automobile? Was it a harvester? Could it fly? The men scratched their heads and stared. Some became excited and waved their arms.

They had heard of little machines like it: the Universal Postal Union, the International Telecommunication Union, the International Institute of Agriculture. A few of the men had actually worked with those little unions.

But this new big one—what could it do?

Let's see what it did do.

At the end of World War I nearly a million refugees from the Russian Revolution were in France, Germany, and other countries. These countries were trying to make them leave because they had no passports.

Hundreds of thousands of European children were starving, many of them homeless, many orphans. This always happens after a war.

In the meetings of the League Council the delegates talked and argued about what to do for these people. The League hired a committee of experts to work for them.

This committee collected information about them, passing this information on to the various governments. At last the League gave passports to many of the refugees and arranged for some countries to let them enter in spite of immigration laws.

Greece and Turkey fought another war, 1921 to 1923. Greece sent home a great many Turks. Vast swarms of refugees crowded into Constantinople.

Turkey expelled 1,400,000 Greeks. They wandered about, starving, in various parts of Greece.

Here the League did some of its best work. It found

jobs for most of the refugees in fifty different countries. It settled 500,000 in new villages all over Greece.

But the League never gave any money, food, clothes, or medicines to refugees. The work it did for children consisted solely of collecting and distributing information.

The reason for this is simple. This big machine—the League of Nations—was so new that the statesmen did not yet know what it could do.

They were like men who had never been in an automobile before, except little toy ones that you pump along with your feet. Now they had a real automobile, the first they had ever seen. They got in. They started the engine. They put it in first gear. "Three cheers!" they shouted. "It works!"

But they had not yet found out that it also had second and high gears and reverse. They found the horn, but they had not yet found the headlights.

So they believed that it could not run at night or go more than ten miles an hour.

They used the League to arrange a private loan of forty million dollars to Greece to help the refugees. But it did not occur to them that the League itself could have handled money.

During World War I German soldiers destroyed many coal mines in the north of France. This habit is one reason why we want to put a stop to wars entirely.

After that war it seemed only fair for France to get some of Germany's coal mines.

But that was not easy. Who lived in the German coal-mining areas? Germans, of course. President Wilson said the people could not be given to France, overlooking the fact that other German-inhabited areas were being given away freely.

So a new way was tried. The victorious Allies carved a section out of Germany and called it the Saar. It was 730 square miles, with 828,000 people. It was crammed full of mines and factories worth a colossal fortune. The Saar was to be ruled by the League of Nations for fifteen years. After that the people must vote whether or not to become part of Germany again.

Could the League rule it? Would the League really give it up after the fifteen years?

The League Council began boldly. It appointed five commissioners from five different countries and sent them to rule the Saar. These five men arrived with seventy-five employees to help them. Also, they had a small army of French soldiers.

The five commissioners hired many local German politicians and policemen. And ordered them to work.

On the first day some of the Germans refused to do as they were told. Obey the League? What was that? Why should they obey it?

The commissioners, with the help of the French soldiers, promptly locked them in jail.

Next day the Germans decided that the League really did have authority. From then on they obeyed.

For fifteen years the League ruled without trouble. The Saar got out of debt, and taxes were lower than in any other place anywhere near there.

Nevertheless the Saar people disliked the League's commissioners, who seemed unable to understand them. In 1935 the League kept its promise to let the Saar people vote. Practically all voted to become part of Germany again.

During World War I Allied armies conquered most of Germany's colonies. They also conquered large parts of the Turkish Empire.

The Covenant of the League of Nations took these places away from the conquerors. Next instant it gave them all back again, but with a difference.

The places were to be called mandates. The conquerors could hold onto them and rule them but must report every year to the Council of the League of Nations.

The ruling nations all promised to take good care of the people in the mandates, to guarantee freedom of religion, to stop the buying and selling of slaves, to control the trade in guns and liquor. They also promised not to build army or navy bases in the mandates.

How well did this system work?

Iraq was mandated to Great Britain, which promised

to let it become independent and free some day. This promise was kept in 1932.

Syria and Lebanon were held by France; Palestine and Trans-Jordan by Great Britain. These also were to become independent. But France and Great Britain would not give them up till they were forced to after World War II.

The Japanese built naval bases (as it had promised not to do) on its mandated islands in the Pacific. The Council of the League heard a rumor about it. They complained. They offered to send a couple of men to look and report whether the rumor was true.

The Japanese simply refused to let the men look. So that was that. The League had no power to insist on an inspection. (Later many American marines were killed rooting out those bases one by one.)

This new machine, the League of Nations, had been built in a hurry. It had gears and headlights, but the clutch often slipped. Some important pieces were entirely missing. One of these missing pieces was the power to inspect the mandates.

The former German colonies in Africa were mandated to Great Britain, France, Belgium, and the Union of South Africa. Sometimes delegates in the League Council scolded one of these nations about its management of a mandated colony. And these scoldings probably did do some good.

Sometimes many people wanted the Council to take

action. It might at least have voted that a ruling country should spend more money in a mandate on public schools or on sewer pipes. But the Council, you remember, could act only by unanimous vote. Well, its members never were unanimous about these questions. Consequently it never did anything at all about any of the mandates.

Woodrow Wilson's original plan for a League of Nations had said that its members should "establish and maintain fair hours and humane conditions of labor."

At the Paris Peace Conference he allowed the foreign statesmen to add several more items of this kind.

So the Covenant said that the League was to try to reduce the slave trade. It should control the selling of opium and other dangerous drugs, supervise the selling of guns, bullets, and bombs. It should help maintain freedom for people to send letters, telegrams, and newspapers to people in other countries, see that each nation gave equal rights to businessmen of all other nations, and try to help prevent diseases.

These ideas were very exciting. When the League began to work, it quickly expanded this brief list.

As no part of the League had been especially designed to do this social welfare work, the job had to be tackled by the Council. The Council passed a few resolutions, but dumped most of the work onto the Secretariat.

They could not do anything about guns, bullets, and bombs.

But they did call a conference of specialists from many countries to discuss the problems of fishermen. They helped get the nations to sign an agreement saying where the various boats would be allowed to fish.

They also called an international conference on passport regulations, another on airplanes, and many others. The result of these conferences was that the nations began to sign agreements about many things they had never agreed about before.

The League created a permanent Advisory Committee on the Traffic in Opium and Other Dangerous Drugs. This committee collected and published a great deal of useful information. For the first time government officials in any country that was trying to control dope peddling could find out where the stuff came from.

The League succeeded in persuading sixty-seven nations to pass laws to control dope. Many governments began to hire inspectors who knew something about it.

This job was so important that it is being continued by the United Nations. Some of the same men and women who did this work for the League are doing it in the new U.N. office.

The League created similar committees to work against the slave trade and for child welfare.

All this was very surprising to the statesmen who had

helped Wilson plan the League. Most of them had thought it would only try to stop wars.

But the big gadget which they had built was able to do more than they had guessed it could. Something very important had gradually come into the world: the new idea that nations could work together on all the common problems and troubles of human life.

The Council of the League invited all the nations to send doctors, hospital managers, and public health officers to a world conference on health.

These people met in April, 1920. They talked about the International Office of Public Health. For thirteen years with not enough money it had been gathering information and showing nations how to fight epidemic diseases. They decided it ought to grow.

So they planned a larger one, the International Health Organization. As this was accepted by many governments, it soon began to work.

It consisted of two parts. One was a large meeting of delegates from the public health offices of many nations, who got together twice a year. They succeeded in writing many agreements about health that the nations later accepted.

The organization consisted, also, of a health section in the League's Secretariat. Here a group of doctors and public health experts worked all year round in offices in Geneva.

At first they thought they would only collect information. And they did collect and hand out a great deal.

But by 1922 the epidemics of cholera, smallpox, malaria, and typhoid left over from the war were getting worse, not better. So the League's International Health Organization began to take real action.

It sent public health experts into Poland. They persuaded the government of Poland to set up delousing shops along the roads. All refugees who passed by had to stop and have their lice removed.

The Health Organization sent many doctors, nurses, and medical students from all over Europe to Greece. They vaccinated half a million refugees. They were particularly successful in stopping typhoid.

At Geneva it built up a special warning service. This grew more active as years passed. (It is still going, now run by the United Nations World Health Organization.) By telegraph and radio this office sent news twice every day, warning doctors and hospitals everywhere of the spread of each disease. The exact movement of each epidemic was charted on maps in colored ink. The central public health office in each country, by watching these maps, could actually see a disease go from one city to the next. They could know in advance whether it was approaching their country.

Joining with others in that world organization meant a lot to a small poor nation. The men in its tiny public health office read the bulletins published by the organization. And in these bulletins they learned all the best sanitary methods yet known anywhere in the world: how to supply doctors and vaccines to public schools without too much expense, how to manage the disposal of sewage and the inspection of travelers.

Actually when the Health Organization of the League of Nations really got going, a great many countries re-organized their public health departments entirely.

Samuel Gompers was a famous labor-union organizer. He was the founder and first president of the American Federation of Labor. In 1918 he went to Paris and badg-ered the delegates at the Peace Conference to do some-thing for working people. He persuaded the diplomats to write a constitution for an International Labor Or-ganization.

As this document was part of the Versailles Treaty, the United States rejected it at first. But the ILO got going in 1920. Fourteen years later the United States joined.

The ILO consisted of three parts: the conference, the governing body, and the office.

Each year all the sixty member nations sent delegates to the conference. Its form was very unusual. Each na-tion sent four people. Two of these represented their government and had to vote as their government wished. The other two voted any way they pleased. One of these represented the labor unions of his country. The other represented the businessmen. These two often voted against each other or against the government delegates from their own country.

In other words, when the 240 delegates voted, labor-union men had a quarter of the votes. Businessmen had a quarter. And governments had half.

The ILO governing body was a committee of thirty-two people. Half were delegates sent by the governments of sixteen nations. Eight others represented business. And eight represented labor.

The ILO also had a secretariat, known as the International Labor Office. It soon consisted of 350 men and women, who worked with the League of Nations at Geneva.

This office collected a great deal of information. It published bulletins and magazines. All over the world these were read in government offices and by employers in business and by labor-union leaders.

Here they got the most up-to-date news of how strikes and labor disputes were handled in different parts of the world. They learned about the latest standards in working conditions, about employers' organizations, about unemployment and what was done to relieve it, about the laws and regulations in all countries concerning accident prevention, safety measures for the sailors on freight boats, social security.

During World War II the International Labor Organization moved temporarily to Montreal in Canada.

Now it is back in Geneva and has become a specialized agency of the United Nations.

At the big annual conferences of the ILO the delegates talk a lot about laws they think the nations ought to have. Frequently they write such a law, and send copies to all the nations. The congress or parliament of each nation may accept it, or it may not. More than half these laws have been accepted by a large number of countries.

These laws have helped many people. When a worker in a South American country breaks a leg and can't work for two months, his children get money from the government insurance fund. The ILO persuaded his government to start that, and showed it how.

A European child can no longer be forced to leave school and work in the coal mines. The ILO persuaded his country to make a law against it.

A British or Norwegian sailor is on a freighter when it is wrecked. In a lifeboat he gets to shore. He has lost his clothes, he is out of a job, he is far from home. What does he do? Beg?

No. The ILO has persuaded his country to establish insurance funds for sailors. He receives his salary, money enough to bring him home, and also the price of new clothes.

However, the ILO has failed on one project. A man who works in a factory making shovels may get a dollar and a half an hour if he is in the United States, half that if he is in England, a third in France, a fifth in Spain, a tenth in India.

Yet they are all in competition with one another. Shovels made in one country can be sold more cheaply than those made in another country.

The best way to protect our own workers from the competition of shovels, shoes, and shears made by poorly paid foreign labor would be to raise the wages of foreign labor up to our level. For thirty years the ILO has been trying to do this. They call it "equal remuneration for work of equal value."

Unfortunately the League of Nations and the ILO had no power. They could not pass any law which employers everywhere would have to accept.

The Council of the League in 1921 appointed a committee of twelve famous scholars—Einstein, Mme. Curie, and ten others.

This committee helped to arrange for a few schoolteachers from one country to be exchanged for a few from another country for a year. They began to help libraries, universities, and research laboratories in different countries to share plans and information.

At first a small office full of men and women of the League Secretariat wrote the letters, kept the records, and did all the practical part of this work. But they soon were swamped with more than they could do.

The French government offered the committee the

use of a palace in Paris and gave them money. When this offer was accepted by the League, the committee became much bigger and was called the Institute of Intellectual Cooperation.

This institute found more and more ways in which nations could help one another's schools, colleges, and scientists.

Now this work has been taken over by the United Nations Educational, Scientific, and Cultural Organization.

When people speak of the League of Nations they usually say that it issued passports to a lot of refugees, that it did good work for the control of dangerous drugs, that it operated an excellent daily warning service on the movement of epidemic diseases, and that it paid for the ILO.

But what did the League do to prevent war?

Well—to answer that question, perhaps we had better start another chapter.

11. *The League Tried to Keep Peace*

As EARLY as 1907 the Second Hague Peace Conference tried to create a world court, but the delegates did not succeed. They wrote a good plan but could not agree on a method for selecting the judges.

But a court was becoming more and more necessary because of the increasing quantity of international law.

Every time a group of delegates from two or more nations sat down together and wrote a treaty, they added to international law. And this was done more and more often. Nations made treaties about more things: about telegrams, railroads, ships, automobile road signs, exchange of money, silk stockings, motion pictures.

Treaties are international law. And customary ways of behaving, such as respecting a flag of truce, are international law. Also former decisions by arbitrators or by courts are used as international law.

And there had come to be so much of this law that an international court was needed to apply it in quarrels between nations.

After World War I the Council of the League of Nations voted to try again to make one. They appointed a committee of ten men who were experts on international law. One was Elihu Root of the United States. During June and July, 1920, these men polished up the same plan.

Elihu Root invented a method for selecting the judges. They would be nominated by the arbitrators on that list of the Permanent Court of Arbitration. Then the nominees would be voted on by the delegates in the League of Nations.

Unfortunately the United States Senate voted against joining the League of Nations and also refused to let the United States join the World Court.

But the court went ahead. In 1922 it began. There were eleven judges at first—later fifteen—working full time. They were paid large salaries by the League of Nations. It was officially entitled the Permanent Court of International Justice. But most people called it the World Court.

In 1931 the government of Norway announced that Norway was taking possession of eastern Greenland. Denmark protested loudly. For centuries both nations had claimed Greenland. Their people became so excited that they seemed about to start fighting a war.

Yet this was entirely a legal question. Who owned eastern Greenland?

That depended on who had explored it, who had settled it, what agreements had been made about it in various treaties. Many nations have claimed newly discovered lands. It is done in a certain way. Customs have been established. These customs have been accepted in regard to northwestern America, Australia, and many other places. Therefore they are international law.

So Denmark and Norway took their quarrel to the World Court. The judges decided in favor of Denmark.[1]

Norway accepted the verdict and withdrew its officers from eastern Greenland.

The court could not order a nation to come in and be tried. It could hear a case only when two nations consented to let it do so.

[1] Our illustrator, then a little boy in Denmark, had a day off from school, as it was a day of national celebration.

During the court's eighteen years it settled thirty-two important cases and many smaller ones. The nations always obeyed the court's verdict.

This is surprising, for the court had no police and no jails.

Greek soldiers marched across the border into Bulgaria in October, 1925.

Next day the chief Bulgarian delegate at Geneva rushed into the office of the Secretary-General of the League.

Clerks in the office telegraphed to the ten nations that were members of the Council. Most of the delegates to the Council were in Paris. So others jumped on trains to get there quickly. (The Council could meet anywhere.) All studied the news reports from the fighting areas.

At 6:00 P.M. on October 26 the Council met. The ten gentlemen frowned at the delegates from Bulgaria, who sat uneasily at one end of the long table, and at the delegates from Greece, who sat at the other end looking a little frightened.

Some very powerful countries were represented in that room: Great Britain, France, Italy, Sweden, Spain, and others. Some of these had recently loaned Greece a lot of money.

Any one country could bring a case to the League Council. This was a big advance over the old system of arbitration. Arbitrators cannot work on a dispute unless both quarreling nations are willing to submit it to them. And very often one is not willing. But Bulgaria alone brought this fight to the League. And if the Bulgars had not done so, some other nation would have, because *any* nation had the right to say to the Council, "Wake up! There's a war starting or about to start!" Then the Council was legally required to go to work on the case.

That night the Council got down to business quickly. They voted on what to do. All members agreed. (The Greeks and Bulgars were not members of the Council, but if they had been they could not have voted anyway, because the Covenant of the League of Nations said the parties to a dispute could not vote.)

The Council sent a telegram to the Greek government "inviting" it to move its soldiers back behind the frontier.

Taking no chances, the Council also voted to send a committee of British, French, and Italian army officers to look and ask questions in both countries and report whether that invitation was obeyed.

And the Council promised to decide after that what should be done.

In Athens the officials decided to obey. They gave orders. The army turned around and marched away. By midnight, October 28, the last invading soldier was back on his own territory. One week had passed since the fight had begun.

In 1920 the League had stopped a quarrel between Sweden and Finland over who should have the Aaland Islands. The islands were near Finland but were inhabited by Swedes.

In 1921 the League settled a dispute between Germany and Poland over who should have Upper Silesia. And in 1932 it prevented a war between Colombia and Peru, who both wanted a little border town called Leticia.

The League never had any power. When it "invited" the Greek government to take the Greek soldiers out of Bulgaria, the world sat around hoping that the Greeks would decide to obey.

The League was most successful when it got delegates from two quarreling nations to sit at the Council's big table and talk things over until a solution was found which both were willing to accept.

Sometimes one country would get an island or a town and would give the other country something in return —maybe the right to go fishing in a certain place, or the privilege of selling sugar to the first country.

But when one of the big, powerful nations went on the warpath, what could the League do to stop it?

On the night of September 18, 1931, Japanese soldiers seized Mukden and several other important cities in northern China.

Two days later the Chinese sent a message to the League, saying, "Please help!"

This was serious, because Japan was one of the big fellows.

When the Council met, the Japanese delegate was, of course, present. Japan was one of the Big Five permanent members. He smilingly explained that the Japanese soldiers were not doing anything naughty. Various Chinese bandit gangs had interfered with important Japanese-owned mines and factories in China. The Japanese soldiers were merely restoring law and order.

After weeks of this talk he himself suggested that the Council should send a commission of inquiry—a group of men to look and ask questions and find out the facts. The Council sent an impressive committee headed by Lord Lytton.

These gentlemen arrived in time to discover that Japanese soldiers had driven the Chinese national army entirely out of Manchuria. They had made Manchuria a separate nation, with a king—who was Chinese. This king was controlled by Japanese advisers.

The Lytton Commission took nine months to write a report. The gentlemen could not agree. Had Japan conquered Manchuria or not? Lord Lytton tried to cut out of the final document most of the points that anyone disliked. Consequently there was not much left in the report. But it did say that Japan was in the wrong.

When at last Lord Lytton gave it to the Council, the delegates seemed to feel uneasy.

Legally if any country—Japan, for instance—went on the warpath, the Council could recommend that all nations take some action. It could recommend that all nations boycott the war-maker. Or the Council could even ask all nations to send guns and soldiers and fight against the offender.

But the Council turned the Lytton report over to the Assembly. The Assembly then had the same powers as the Council but with this big advantage: in the Assembly all member nations were represented. They were all independent sovereign nations. The diplomats thought there was no point in asking all those nations to do anything without first finding out whether they would all vote for it. That was the theory of national sovereignty at that time.

However, in the Assembly any nation could veto a whole proposal.

The Lytton report was mimeographed, and copies were handed to all the delegates in the Assembly at Geneva. The delegates met, discussed, argued.

Some wanted to boycott Japan. This was called voting "sanctions" against it. Others said, "But if we stop selling things to Japan, our countries will lose money." Not merely a little money. A great deal of money. Japan was an industrial country with many factories, many ships.

Also Japan was very powerful, with a large army and navy. Nobody even wanted to mention the idea of sending soldiers and guns to fight against it.

So the delegates looked at one another and sighed.

In February, 1933, after the Japanese had begun to advance southward from Manchuria to take some more of China, the Assembly at last voted. They "adopted" the Lytton report, which scolded Japan. That was all.

The Japanese militarists must have smiled.

Japan had tried aggression and had not been punished. So the government leaders in Italy and Germany opened their eyes wide, shrugged their shoulders, and asked, "Why don't we try it too?"

Mussolini, the Fascist dictator of Italy, made speeches saying Italy must become a great empire. On October 3, 1935, his soldiers in tanks and airplanes plowed into Ethiopia.

Both countries were members of the League. The Ethiopian delegates at Geneva immediately demanded action.

For the first and only time in its entire history the League of Nations tried to do something.

The Council met quickly. Within four days it voted, declaring that Italy was an aggressor. It turned the case over to the Assembly for action.

The Assembly met at once. For four days the delegates argued. Should they vote that all nations must refuse to sell weapons or ammunition to Italy? Yes. Must refuse to loan Italy any money? Yes. Must stop buying anything at all from Italy? Well, that was difficult. Olive oil, spaghetti, wine— They voted: Yes, stop buying from Italy. How about selling raw materials to Italy? Must be stopped—iron, copper, coal, rubber. Oil?

What about oil?

Italy had already bought large quantities of iron, copper, coal, rubber. Italian factories had already made cannons, machine guns, poison gas, tanks, airplanes, trucks. The army did not need any more. But to run those airplanes, tanks, trucks, ships, Italy would need a steady supply of oil.

The delegates telegraphed home to their governments for last-minute instructions.

The French premier, Pierre Laval, whispered to his friends, "If we really stop Mussolini, he may become angry and join Hitler against us. We had better let him have the oil."

Out loud the French delegates argued, "The United States is the largest producer of oil in the world, and it is not a member of the League. No matter what we do, it will keep on selling oil to Mussolini. So why should we stop? Our oil companies would lose money, while United States companies would take our business."

Was this true? If the League Assembly, representing fifty-five nations, had sent a strong appeal to President Franklin D. Roosevelt asking the United States to join in the boycott against war-making Fascist Italy, would he and the United States Congress have cooperated? We don't know. The League never tried it.

On October 11, 1935, the Assembly voted sanctions against Italy, boycotting everything—except oil.

Italy bought more and more oil. The Fascist army made full use of airplanes and poison gas. The Ethiopians had only a swarm of brave men and a few rifles. Yet the tanks and planes took seven months to reach the capital city, Addis Ababa. Then the war was over.

So was the League. On May 5, 1936, Addis Ababa fell, and the League of Nations was dead.

World organization had grown quite a bit since the first International Telegraph Union in 1865. Within sixty years it had reached the point of telling Greek soldiers to get out of Bulgaria. In 1925 the Greeks obeyed.

But that world organization was still only a committee of sovereign nations. It had no power to arrest men. It could not put Japanese military leaders or Mussolini in jail.

It could only boycott an entire nation. A boycott would punish innocent Japanese or Italian children by wrecking the businesses where their fathers worked. This would also cause other League member nations to lose money. So the member nations did not like to do it.

And they played their old game of politics. *We can't*

stop Mussolini; he might become angry and join Hitler against us.

The League of Nations was an experiment. It was the first attempt at a world organization large enough to keep peace. And it was a failure.

Big important things always begin that way. The first attempt is always a failure. Maybe the second and third attempts will fail, too. We don't yet know what the United Nations can do. But if people keep learning and keep improving the method, it can grow until it will be strong enough to succeed.

12. *World War II Produced the U.N.*

In July, 1936, civil war began in Spain. Mussolini and Hitler sent soldiers, tanks, airplanes, bombs, to help the fascist rebel, General Franco. The Russians sent bullets and advisers to help the popularly elected Spanish government.

The League of Nations appointed a committee to study the war. That was all the League did about it.

120

The war lasted two and a half years. All over Spain farms, villages, cities were destroyed. Over five per cent of the people were killed or driven out of the country. The fascists won.

Hitler, the Nazi dictator of Germany, had a large, powerful army. In March, 1938, his soldiers stormed into Austria. They made it part of Germany. The League did nothing.

Pleased with this success, Hitler sent his soldiers to take part of Czechoslovakia. Both the Council and the Assembly of the League were meeting at the time. But although Czechoslovakia was a member, the Czechs did not even bother to appeal to the League. What was the use?

After another six months Hitler took all the rest of Czechoslovakia. Why not? He wanted it, and obviously no one was going to stop him.

A few days later, in April, 1939, Mussolini sent his soldiers to Albania. They seized the whole country. The League did nothing.

By the middle of the summer anyone could see that Hitler and Mussolini would keep on grabbing places. They had taken Ethiopia, put their puppet in Spain, seized Austria, Czechoslovakia, and Albania, while the Japanese were conquering China.

In August Hitler announced that there was a quarrel between him and Poland. Should the other nations wave good-by to Poland also?

The world had methods for settling quarrels peacefully. President Roosevelt sent telegrams to Hitler and to the president of Poland. He asked them to end their dispute by one of these four methods: diplomacy, mediation, a commission of inquiry, or arbitration.

The Polish president cabled back that his government would be glad to settle the quarrel peacefully. He accepted Roosevelt's offer to mediate.

But mediation cannot begin till both parties accept it. Would Hitler accept it?

No one could make him. Other nations could only ask him to. According to the old theory of national sovereignty a nation could, if it chose, submit to mediation, to arbitration, or to the World Court. But outsiders must not try to force it to do so.

The League of Nations had gone beyond that motheaten old theory. The League could discuss Hitler's quarrel regardless of whether he was willing or not. The League could even do something about it—provided that all member nations agreed.

But the League did nothing.

And on September 1, 1939, Hitler marched his soldiers into Poland.

Someone had to stop him. Great Britain and France sent him warnings. He paid no attention. Two days later Great Britain and France declared war against Germany.

World War II had begun.

The Germans, under Hitler, had set out to conquer all Europe. Hitler planned that all non-German people must become serfs or slaves and work for the Germans. He planned that after he had conquered Europe he would take control of the whole world, making Asia and America his colonies.

That sounds crazy, but he very nearly succeeded.

In three weeks his armies conquered Poland. Next April he conquered Denmark and Norway, then The Netherlands, Belgium, Luxembourg. In May his armies invaded France. Within a few weeks they had practically destroyed the French armies.

Because Hitler was winning, Mussolini decided to join him in the war. The Italian soldiers marched a few miles into France, giving it the famous "stab in the back." This was France's reward for all its efforts to keep friendly with the Italians during the League of Nations debates over Italy's invasion of Ethiopia. This sort of behavior has been typical of international relations. So long as the nations remain sovereign, independent, believing that they can do as they please, they never act like real friends.

On June 16, 1940, at the climax of the Battle for France, the British government offered to merge itself with the French government. "Every citizen of France will enjoy immediate citizenship of Great Britain," said the official telegram from London. "Every British subject will become a citizen of France." The members of the French National Assembly would immediately become members of the British Parliament.

The two nations would become one. United, they would continue to fight Germany.

But this extraordinary offer was not accepted. The French government officials knew that their army was beaten. They only wanted to make peace with Germany.

Yet the offer will not be forgotten. In another time of danger the same nations or others may seek safety by uniting.

That time the offer came too late. The German armies had already gone too far. A few days later the French government surrendered to Hitler in the same railway car near Versailles in which the Germans had surrendered to the French at the end of World War I, twenty-two years before.

Hitler now had a fool for an ally—Mussolini, the dictator of Italy. Mussolini sent Italian armies into Greece, and they were promptly and entirely defeated. So Hitler had to send a German army to rescue them. After that the Italians did very little in the war, except that a few of them trotted along with the much larger German armies. The rest of the war in Europe was fought by Germany almost entirely alone against the world.

The Germans conquered not only Greece but also

Hungary, Rumania, Bulgaria, Yugoslavia. They also took most of North Africa.

Throughout the winter of 1940–1941 Hitler sent his airplanes to attack England, bombing the cities and trying to destroy the British air force. This was the great Battle of Britain.

But English factories went all-out in making airplanes. A great many planes were flown in from the United States. And the British air force won. It was Hitler's first major defeat.

Late in June, 1941, the German armies marched into Russia. They seized a great deal of it. For hundreds of miles they advanced so rapidly that they seemed about to defeat the Soviet Union completely.

Hitler had conquered all Europe. He could use all its mines and factories and workmen to build up his military power. Little England would then be alone against him.

At that moment President Franklin D. Roosevelt of the United States and Prime Minister Winston Churchill of Great Britain sailed out on battleships and met in the Atlantic Ocean.

Together they wrote and signed the Atlantic Charter on August 14, 1941. It said that the two countries expected some day the establishment of a world organization to keep peace.

They were not alone in this idea. The following

winter on December 4 Premier Stalin signed a treaty with the Polish government-in-exile. They demanded a union of democratic states to uphold international law and keep peace.

Three days later Japan entered the war. The Japanese militarists set out to conquer all Asia. They began December 7, 1941, by a furious sneak attack against the United States Navy at Pearl Harbor in Hawaii.

Germany and Italy immediately declared war against the United States.

Within two weeks nine of the smallest and nearest Latin-American countries gave their answer by declaring war against Germany and Japan.

A few days later, on January 1, 1942, representatives from the twenty-six allied countries met at Washington. Here were men from the Big Four—the United States, Great Britain, the Soviet Union, China—and the five great countries of the British Commonwealth of Nations, and those nine Latin-American republics. All these countries were at war against Germany, Italy, and Japan. Also came men from eight European countries occupied by the Nazis.

All twenty-six signed a declaration saying they agreed with the Atlantic Charter, pledging themselves to cooperate in the struggle against Hitlerism, and proudly calling themselves "the United Nations."

They were not united at all. This was only talk.

But it was brave talk, and it was followed slowly by

action. Once before, on a summer day in wartime in 1776, thirteen states had called themselves "the United States of America." They had not been united at all. But thirteen years later they became united.

And that winter day in wartime in 1942 those first twenty-six nations called themselves "the United Nations."

The Japanese captured the Philippine Islands, the Dutch East Indies, and Singapore. Thailand (Siam) joined them as allies. The Japanese defeated the British and Chinese forces in Burma, took Rangoon and Mandalay. Meanwhile they were grabbing large parts of China. They captured many islands in the Pacific Ocean.

Together the Germans and Japanese had conquered all Europe and most of the richest parts of Asia. Supplying their armies by means of the captured factories and captured mines and oil wells, they were ten times more powerful than when the war had begun.

Yet after six months of fighting, the United States Navy and Air Force defeated the Japanese navy in great battles in the Coral Sea and at Midway. In August, 1942, the Americans seized Guadalcanal and began to capture one island at a time across the Pacific, stepping stones to Japan.

The Russians at Stalingrad at last halted the German army thirteen hundred miles from Germany. In November with large quantities of weapons sent from the United States the Red Army began a long, bloody counterattack, driving the Germans back home.

United States and British armies landed in North Africa. All winter they advanced slowly. In July, 1943, they invaded Sicily, then Italy.

The tide of war had turned. Would victory produce a world organization to prevent another?

President Roosevelt and Prime Minister Churchill had written the Atlantic Charter, demanding a world organization to keep peace. Stalin had signed a treaty with Poland, demanding one. Twenty-six nations had agreed with the Atlantic Charter. Both the Democratic and Republican parties in the United States had asked for it. Many writers, public speakers, and organizations were demanding it too.

President Roosevelt wanted to go ahead and make one, perhaps like the League of Nations—or, if possible, better. But he had read about the mistake President Wilson had made. Wilson wrote most of the Covenant of the League of Nations himself and forgot to find out whether the Senate of the United States would accept it.

Therefore President Roosevelt began by talking the idea over with Senators and representatives in Congress. In September, just after the surrender of Italy, the

House of Representatives voted that the United States ought to join a world organization to keep peace.

The United States Secretary of State, Cordell Hull, spent eleven days in Moscow talking with the Foreign Secretaries of Great Britain and the Soviet Union, Anthony Eden and Vyacheslav M. Molotov. Toward the end of their meetings they called in the Chinese ambassador.

On November 1 these representatives of the Big Four nations signed the Moscow Declaration, saying they "recognize the necessity of establishing at the earliest practicable date a general international organization" to keep peace. They wanted "all peace-loving states" to join it.

Right away the United States Senate debated this declaration. The Senate had rejected the League of Nations. Uneasily the whole world waited to hear what the Senators would decide this time.

Five days later they voted 85 to 5 in favor of joining such an organization.

The plan had not yet been written. President Roosevelt knew better than to write it himself. It was too big a thing to be made by one person.

Instead he appointed a committee of men from both houses of Congress and from the State Department. They worked for many months, writing a blueprint for a world organization.

They did not have to begin with nothing. For centuries people had been writing these plans, all the way from Pierre Dubois' book in the year 1306 to the League of Nations. Better still, the League had tried out its plan in actual experience. The committee could see which parts of the League plan had worked and which parts had not.

After several months the committee handed a new plan to the President. He sent copies to Great Britain, China, and the Soviet Union.

Government committees in those countries had been working, too. Within a few days they all sent back plans of their own.

The next step was to see if those four plans could be put together to make one. Two important conferences tried to do it, at Dumbarton Oaks and at Yalta.

Most of the countries in the world joined the so-called United Nations in the final assault of the war.

They sent great fleets of heavy bombing planes over Germany and Japan both night and day. Often a thousand planes at once would attack a city, sometimes two thousand. Better bombs were invented and used.

The whole character of war changed completely from what it had been. In the old days war had been a fight between a group of armed men on one side and another group of armed men on the other side.

But by 1944 war had become a scientific slaughter

and destruction of whole cities by machines flying overhead. Men, women, children were murdered. Houses were burned and exploded until block after block, street after street were changed to rocky deserts worse than the Sahara. Schools, grocery stores, clothing stores, factories, warehouses—everything built by man—were bombed out. Public libraries, hospitals, police stations, jails, churches, fire-engine stations, public water works, theaters—all destroyed.

In June, 1944, soldiers of the United States, England, and Canada landed in the north of France. They began rapidly to grind the German armies to pieces, while the Russians far away drove the Germans out of the last great city of Russia.

When the Dumbarton Oaks Conference began in August, 1944, the Allies, joined by a small Free French army, were marching into Paris. U.S. soldiers were dying by the thousands, driving the Germans slowly northward through the mountains of Italy. In the hot, steaming south Pacific they were hopping dangerously from island to island toward Japan.

Dumbarton Oaks is a beautiful mansion on an estate in Washington, D.C. Seventeen delegates of the United States met the delegations from England, the Soviet Union, and China.

Together they set to work to find out whether they could mold their four plans for a world organization into one on which their four governments would agree. The

League's experience had showed that a world organization was greatly weakened if one of the biggest nations stayed out. Therefore the men tried very hard to make a plan that all four big nations would accept.

For a month and a half the men worked. And they squeezed their four plans into one, called the Dumbarton Oaks Proposals.

Millions of copies were printed. People all over the world studied it. All the governments of the smaller countries began to prepare their ideas for improving it.

There were some gaps in it. The diplomats at Dumbarton Oaks especially could not agree on how much power each nation ought to have in the Security Council.

Next February, in the last winter of the war, three men met at Yalta in the southern part of Russia: President Roosevelt in his long warm cape; Prime Minister Churchill, round faced, with a cigar; Marshal Stalin with heavy moustache, wearing a soldier's cap.

Even these men had trouble. Roosevelt knew there was no use in his agreeing to anything that the Senate would not accept later on. So he had to consult his advisers about every point that was discussed.

They were not going to make the mistake again of letting every little country have a veto in the Security Council, as in the League of Nations. But the United States Senate wanted the U.S.A. to have a veto. The Senate would insist on it. The Russians also wanted a veto and would insist on it. Neither of these big countries would join the organization at all if they did not each have a veto.

So at Yalta they compromised. The big nations would have the veto in the Security Council. But they would do without it in the General Assembly.

The small nations would not have any veto. They might not like this, but it was the only answer that both the Senate and the Kremlin would accept.

At last, after all this work, a new world organization really seemed possible. So the governments of the four big nations invited all the countries that had signed the United Nations Declaration to send delegates to a conference at San Francisco to complete the plan.

This invitation went only to nations that had declared war against Germany or Japan. Suddenly the countries of South America and the Near East were stirred to action. The conference was going to be important. Ten more nations declared war on Germany and Japan in time to be invited. Fifty nations took part in the conference.

The day the four hundred delegates met in the San Francisco Opera House, April 25, 1945, the Russian army encircled Berlin. They fought the Nazis a nightmare battle down in the fifty miles of subway tunnels under the city. That same day American soldiers coming from the west and Soviet soldiers coming from the east met and shook hands in the middle of Germany, while American marines fought a slow, costly advance on Okinawa Island close to Japan.

Each of the fifty national delegations arrived well prepared with official papers, with ideas, and with advisers, lawyers, and translators. The only bright spots visible were the turbans of the delegates from India and the white headdresses from Arabia. Four thousand people crowded into the opera house. But there was no cheering, no excited speechmaking. These people had come to work, not to make a noise.

The delegates divided up into committees. One committee worked for weeks on the plan for a Security Council. Another worked on the Trusteeship Council. There was a committee for every part of the new charter.

Every national delegation brought its own ideas for changing the Dumbarton Oaks plan or at least for adding to it. The delegation from Australia, for example, handed in thirty-eight definite amendments. Actually twenty-six of these were put into the charter.

While they worked to build an organization to keep peace, Hitler's body was soaked in gasoline and set on fire in a bomb shelter deep under the ruins of Berlin. At last the remnants of the German army's high command surrendered. The war in Europe was over.

While the delegates worked in San Francisco, vast areas in Tokyo were burned out by United States air raids. Okinawa Island was conquered.

When the committees at San Francisco had done

everything they could to improve their parts of the plan, all the parts were worked together into one document called the Charter of the United Nations.

On June 26 all the chief delegates signed it. Printed copies were then sent to their governments, which could accept it or reject it.

The United States Senate had rejected the League of Nations. After a heated debate, the Senate voted that the United States would officially accept the U.N. Times had changed. On the very day while they were voting, the first atomic bomb was exploded in a test over a desert in New Mexico.

Two weeks later—August 6, 1945—the worst weapon ever made, the atomic bomb, was dropped on Hiroshima in Japan. Sixty-six thousand people were killed, most of them by burns, the rest by falling pieces of buildings and flying glass. Four square miles of buildings were knocked down.

Eight days later the Japanese emperor spoke to his people by radio. He announced that they were surrendering. World War II was over.

All round the world orphans and widows mourned for the twenty-two million dead. And over thirty-four million men, women, and children had been wounded.

War was becoming more and more expensive. The armies and weapons in the Second World War had cost four times as much as in the first. And we can't even estimate the far greater cost of the enormous destruction of cities and factories and oil wells and mines.

Ever since war was invented by the apes, it has been growing worse and worse.

One by one the governments of the fifty-one victorious nations officially accepted the Charter of the United Nations.

By October 24 enough acceptances had been recorded to put the Charter into force as a part of international law.

After three more months of preparation the organization came to life on a cold, drizzling afternoon, January 10, 1946, when the first General Assembly met in London. The Security Council, the Secretariat, and the other branches of the U.N. got down to business.

Can it succeed where the League of Nations failed?

13. *How the United Nations Works*

Is THE United Nations a step forward? Is it better than the League?

In the League the largest number of nations ever represented in the Assembly at once was fifty-five.

In the U.N. the original members in 1945 were: the Big Five (the United States, Great Britain, France, China, and the Soviet Union); the Ukraine and Byelo-

russia; the five great dominions of the British Commonwealth of Nations; twenty Latin-American countries;
nine small European countries; seven Moslem countries around Asia Minor; two African countries (Ethiopia and Liberia); and the Philippines. Fifty-one.

Nine more soon got in: Iceland, Sweden, Israel, Ye-
men, Afghanistan, Pakistan, Burma, Thailand, Indonesia. All together: sixty.

So the U.N. was bigger than the League. And it can
grow bigger still. Fourteen more countries knocked at
the door, asking to be let in. Nine of them were vetoed
by Russia, five by other big nations in the Security
Council. But the door should open.

The League had a Secretariat of about 630 people.
The U.N. usually has over 3,500. During meetings of
the General Assembly the U.N. has many more. It needs
all these people because it is doing more than the
League ever did.

The League consisted of a Council, an Assembly, a
Secretariat. It also had the International Labor Organization and the World Court. The U.N. has all these and
more besides.

The U.N. Security Council resembles the Council of
the League. Each has consisted of the Big Five plus a
batch of little countries. Every country that is a member
of the Council sends one delegate to sit at the Council
table.

The Big Five are permanent members. The little

countries change, as they are elected from time to time by the Assembly.

The Big Five keep changing, too. The League was to have had the United States, Great Britain, France, Italy, and Japan. But it began without the United States. So at first it had only a Big Four. Then in 1926 Germany joined. So the League had a Big Five at last. In 1934 the Soviet Union joined, making the Big Six. In 1935 Germany and Japan angrily dropped out from the League entirely. So it ended with a Big Four again.

The U.N. began with five permanent members in the Security Council: the United States, Great Britain, France, the Soviet Union, and China. Probably this list will soon be changed again.

In the League Assembly every member nation could have three delegates but only one vote.

In the U.N. General Assembly each nation can send five delegates plus five alternates (usually these ten people sit together) and each nation has one vote.

All these ten people are needed because the U.N. General Assembly has so many committees and subcommittees. A number of committees argue in different rooms on the same afternoon at 3:00 P.M.

In fact, there is so much work to do that when the ten people from the United States arrived in Paris for the 1951 meeting, they brought a hundred assistants with them.

The U.N. General Assembly also has the help of two

more councils which the League did not have. These are very useful.

The Economic and Social Council (known as EcoSoc) consists of eighteen member nations, elected by the General Assembly. Each sends one delegate.

EcoSoc studies reports from all the huge specialized agencies. They are trying to get food for hungry people, teach a billion illiterates to read and write, stop diseases all over the world, and help everyone to get a job and a home.

And EcoSoc has many committees of its own and special commissions in their own offices in various parts of the globe.

The U.N. also has a Trusteeship Council. This consists of twelve nations. The Big Five are in. Australia, Belgium, and New Zealand are in because they govern certain colonies for the U.N. Four more countries are elected by the General Assembly. The arithmetic is planned so that the number of countries in the Trusteeship Council that don't govern colonies will equal the number that do.

This council studies reports from its members who govern colonies in trusteeship for the U.N. It also demands reports from all nations concerning all colonies. And it scolds them when necessary. It does a good deal to help colonial people who are not governing themselves. It works on the theory that it is going to make them all independent pretty soon, and thereby put itself out of existence.

The U.N. has a World Court—almost exactly the same as the League's.

The U.N. also has ten specialized agencies. Here is a list, telling how many nations were members of each agency in 1951:

> *International Telecommunication Union* (this is the oldest) 81 nations
>
> *Universal Postal Union* (this is the largest) 86 nations
>
> *World Health Organization* (WHO) 78 nations
>
> *International Labor Organization* (ILO) 64 nations
>
> *Food and Agriculture Organization of the United Nations* (FAO) 66 nations
>
> *United Nations Educational, Scientific, and Cultural Organization* (UNESCO) 64 nations
>
> *International Civil Aviation Organization,* 57 nations
>
> *World Meteorological Organization* (this is the youngest) 35 nations
>
> *International Bank,* 50 nations
>
> *International Monetary Fund,* 50 nations

There have been others. For example, the United Nations Relief and Rehabilitation Administration

(UNRRA) and the International Refugee Organization (IRO) did a great deal for refugees. And there probably will be more of these big agencies.

Each specialized agency has a conference from time to time, when delegates from all its member nations get together. Each agency also has a steering committee or council that meets more often. And each has a secretariat of its own. Together they employ over four thousand people and have office buildings in many cities.

The League usually spent about $6,000,000 a year. (Two years its expenses reached $6,500,000.)

The U.N. has been spending over $48,000,000 a year.

Of the specialized agencies the first eight on our list together have spent about $31,000,000 a year. (The Bank and the Fund earn more than they spend.)

In one typical year, 1950, the U.N. also spent $40,000,000 on aid to Palestine refugees, $35,000,000 for European refugees, $20,000,000 on aid to children, and $20,000,000 on technical help to underdeveloped countries. Total: $214,000,000.

Obviously the U.N. is much bigger and a great deal more serious than the League ever was.

Does the U.N. expense seem too large? You have to multiply that total by 500 to find how much the U.N. member nations were spending for weapons and soldiers.

The League of Nations *could* use force. But it never did.

The U.N. actually sent soldiers to Korea to fight against an army of aggressors.

Is this morally better than what the League did? You must answer this question yourself.

At least it means that the U.N. has to be taken seriously. It has to be taken much more seriously than the League.

In the Council of the League every nation, large or small, could defeat any proposal by merely saying, "No." This is called having a veto.

In the Security Council of the U.N. only the Big Five have the veto. Eleven nations are represented in it. Decisions are made by majority of at least seven, provided that all the Big Five are among those seven. (This is a trifle less than a two-thirds majority.)

In the General Assembly any important decision can be made if approved by two-thirds of the nations that vote. If all sixty vote, any forty votes are enough. No one has a veto.

The United States has often had to accept decisions made in the General Assembly when it had voted against them.

This means that the old theory of national sovereignty has at last been seriously changed. When you are a member of a club, you have to accept the decisions of the majority. That is fair play. At last the nations have admitted that they must play fair, too.

This is by far the most important advance that the United Nations has made over the League.

This is the United Nations.
What has it actually done?

14. *The U.N. Helps People in Trouble*

WHEN YOU live in a country that is fighting a big war, you can't get much meat to eat. You notice that the grocer does not have enough paper bags. He asks you to bring a bag of your own. There are shortages of automobile tires, cigarettes, nylon stockings.

But when the war comes closer, bombs fall on your city. With roaring explosions the railroad stations topple into ruin. The bombs flatten out department stores, houses, hospitals. Then you cannot get new clothes. Fuel is rationed, and all winter your home is chilly. Each week some of your friends are killed.

And when the battle line grinds across your town, your grocer cannot get food at all. Somehow you manage to find a few potatoes perhaps, some carrots, a can of beans once in a while. Every day you are hungry. In winter your broken house has no heat. It is just as cold as outdoors.

Then if you become sick no doctor calls to see you. When the neighbors are sick they cannot reach any doctor either. Yet if you find a cabbage that is not clean or fresh you are so hungry you have to eat it—knowing that if it makes you ill you will have no doctor. The drugstore has sold all its medicines. There are no more.

Soon most of the people are sick. Some die. Some just stay sick. It is hard to get well when you are starving.

The diseases last longer than the war. In World War I and in the first years after it the ten million people who died of sickness and hunger were more than those killed by bullets and bombs.

In World War II the bullets and bombs were more efficient, slaughtering twenty-two million. Hitler's extermination camps murdered at least eight million more. The ten million who starved to death or were victims of disease this time seem not so many by comparison.

What has the world done for these victims of war?

The Hoover Commission for Relief in Belgium in 1914 to 1919 distributed food, medicine, clothes, blankets, and other useful things worth over $1,300,000,-000.

As soon as the war ended, in November, 1918, Mr. Hoover headed the American Relief Administration. It gave food to all countries in Europe, including the enemy. In one year it spent $1,150,000,000.

Most of this came from the United States. Ten per cent came from England. Several other countries gave a little.

This all ended before the League of Nations began.

During World War II the governments decided to handle war relief by means of the great new method of international organization. The method had been in use quite a while. Politicians at last had some notion how to work it.

In November, 1943, delegates from forty-four nations met in a big room at Atlantic City. They created the United Nations Relief and Rehabilitation Administration (UNRRA).

It was organized in the usual way. In its big council each member nation had one vote. (This council met six times.) And the secretariat consisted of a Director-general and many employees. At one time UNRRA had a staff of 24,000 men and women, who came from fifty different countries.

As soon as the U.N. came into existence as a real organization, UNRRA became connected to it.

UNRRA tried to do a better job than had ever been done before. Instead of giving mostly food, it gave food and also a lot of plows, farm tractors, and seed. It helped farmers to begin raising crops and cows again.

Instead of giving just clothes and blankets, it gave clothes and blankets and also a lot of looms, sewing machines, and big engines. It helped factories to begin making clothes and blankets again.

Then the people could get jobs. This was the most important of all. They got jobs on the farms and in the factories and could earn a living.

UNRRA distributed goods worth $3,970,000,000.

To several million war refugees UNRRA meant food, blankets in winter, beds, houses in which to find shelter. Some families wandered helpless in the streets because their homes had been bombed or destroyed by cannons. Others would not go back to Poland, Czechoslovakia, or the other countries conquered by the communists.

UNRRA took leftover prisoner-of-war camps, army training camps that were no longer being used, and concentration camps. The refugees themselves tore down the barbed wire, cleaned out the dormitories, lighted fires in the kitchen stoves. The refugees themselves organized little hospitals in the camps and schools for the children. UNRRA supplied medicines and books.

UNRRA soon found jobs and homes for one million of these people.

When UNRRA went out of existence in September, 1948, a new organization took over. It was the United Nations International Refugee Organization (IRO). Eighteen nations were members.

IRO got a fleet of ships and carried another million refugees to the United States, Latin America, Israel, and the British dominions.

The one-millionth refugee resettled by IRO was a Catholic man from Czechoslovakia. With his wife and two daughters he had fled when their little country was taken by the Red Army. IRO brought them to the United States, where the man got a job on a farm in Texas. His older daughter, a handsome girl twenty-one years old, planned to study dress designing. The other, who was ten, would go to school.

Wars and oppressions drove other hundreds of thousands of men, women, and children from their homes in Palestine, Greece, Korea. Thousands in Italy wanted to leave because they could not find jobs.

In one year the U.N. spent $67,000,000 on relief in Korea. Thailand and the Philippines sent rice. Israel gave sulfa drugs. In Seoul in Korea housewives stood in line beside the destroyed buildings and had their shopping bags filled with rice by local officials working for the U.N.

When the IRO ended in 1952, smaller U.N. committees took over the work, with IRO's fleet of ships. Experts said there would still be refugees for many years.

The League of Nations had never spent a penny of money on direct help to anyone. It gave legal help, gave passports, gave advice. It found jobs for refugees. It gathered facts for governments and for private charities.

The U.N. has gone much further. It even has a special fund for emergency relief. In February, 1951, the General Assembly voted to take $5,000,000 from this fund and spend it on the people uprooted by the war in Palestine. Food and clothes began to reach the starving, penniless Arab refugees before the much larger program of U.N. help for them had time to get going.

A yellow-haired young boy in Sweden and a black-haired young girl in Ceylon were vaccinated against tuberculosis. Four years later they still had not caught the disease, though in previous years many children in their villages used to catch it.

The wooden cases full of bottles of vaccine were labeled UNICEF, meaning the United Nations International Children's Emergency Fund. Seventeen million children were vaccinated.

In the first years after the war, mules, men, and trucks carried UNICEF's cardboard boxes of powdered milk, shoes, coats, and medicines to children in war-devastated villages.

UNICEF accepts money from anyone who will give

any. Governments have given the most. Money comes also from churches, from schools, from businessmen, from children.

Greek boys and girls in villages destroyed by civil war ran out to meet the trucks bringing UNICEF milk, clothes, shoes.

In Latin America, Afghanistan, and Burma, UNICEF has taught nurses how to teach mothers to care for their children's health more scientifically.

Over 42,000,000 children in sixty different countries are healthier and less hungry thanks to the work of this fund. But many more are still hungry, homeless, neglected. More money for many years will be needed.

Sir Benegal Rau, chief delegate from India to the U.N., received a letter written by three children in the United States.

> *Dear Mr. Rau,*
> *Yesterday we three were hungry and shared a banana. We thanked God for food. Then we remembered that Indian children needed food. What could we do about it? Mary, aged three, held out the rest of her share of the banana. "Here," she said. We told her that bananas wouldn't keep fresh all the way to India. And so we are now sending this bit to you to buy wheat for the children of India with our hearts full of sympathy for them in their trouble.*

Enclosed was a postal money order for one dollar.

On a farm in Africa two oxen used to pull the plow. But the animals died of a disease called rinderpest. Next day the farmer stood looking at the plow. What could he do? If he did not plow his field and plant seed, he would get no crop, and his family would starve.

So he did as thousands of other farmers were doing. He and his wife and their oldest son and daughter put the harness on their shoulders and pulled the plow, sweating and groaning with the hard labor.

In many parts of Africa and Asia rinderpest in one year killed nine out of every ten cows and oxen.

FAO, the U.N. agency for farmers, did research, found a vaccine to prevent that disease. FAO sent men to teach the Africans, Afghans, Indians, and Burmese to use the vaccine.

Often the farmers were afraid of the white man's magic. FAO had to hire more teachers and try again.

FAO collected facts and for the first time found out how many people were hungry. Sixty per cent of the people in the world in 1951 had "insufficient nutrition." That means that more than half of us did not get enough to eat.

And hunger was growing worse, not better. From 1936 to 1951 the number of people in the world increased 13 per cent. But food production increased only 9 per cent.

Hundreds of millions of men and women who were hungry all the time and who saw their children grow sick from lack of food, were becoming hungrier. What would they do? Fight? Kill a few rich people? Join communist revolts? Why not?

FAO introduced better kinds of wheat, oats, and rye into Europe. It taught Haitians to raise fish in pond nurseries. It sent a stronger breed of sheep to Afghanistan.

FAO began a blitz attack against locusts. (A locust is a grasshopper, only hungrier.) When the usual great swarms of locusts swoop down to eat up the entire crops of nations, twenty-five FAO airplanes swoop down too, spraying insect poison.

Much of FAO's work is research. It finds out what kinds of wheat and what breeds of cows, pigs, and chickens are best for each climate. Latin-American farmers were given shovels. The men could not use them. Bare feet or sandals cannot push shovels. So FAO sent hoes instead.

FAO workers showed farmers in Asia how to get more grain from the land by using steel plows instead of wooden ones.

And still the people were becoming hungrier and hungrier. FAO has done good work, but it has had only $5,000,000 a year. That was one dollar a year for every 260 hungry people.

How much is $5,000,000? In 1950 the people of

the United States spent $749,000,000 on cosmetics. Surely we could spend a little more on FAO's fight for food.

A young man in Haiti received a steamship ticket, paid for by the U.N. He traveled to France (Haitians speak French). There he studied in a school of agriculture. The U.N. paid for his tuition and his room and meals. He learned modern methods of irrigation.

Next year he was back in Haiti, squinting one eye and waving his hands as he looked through a surveyor's telescope. He was leading a crew of workmen on a big irrigation project to bring water into a dry valley. Soon the valley would be green with fields of beans and cabbages for hungry Haitians.

Twenty-six experts sent by the U.N. arrived in the beautiful mountain city of Bogotá in Colombia in South America. Soon some were at work in the government offices. Others set out for the small towns.

One showed the officials how to collect facts about prices of food, hats, shoes, and other things sold in the stores. He drew charts and showed how these facts about prices could be useful. When prices go up, something is wrong, and the government should know it. When prices go down, taxes must go down; so the government had better be watching then, too.

Other experts studied the country for weeks, then wrote plans, showing how schools could be made more interesting to the children. The experts also planned improvements in hospitals, airports, banks.

The government of Colombia paid half their expenses. The U.N. paid the other half.

The U.N. believes that this is better than charity. Many countries are so poor that even the best workmen can scarcely earn enough to live on, and their children are ragged, hungry, and unable to read. But richer countries should not merely send a little money. It is better to send a team of experts to show those countries how to help themselves.

This idea went into action in 1949, when the U.N. General Assembly voted to launch its big program of technical aid. This consists of two main parts. (1) The U.N. sends experts to underdeveloped countries. (2) The U.N. pays for young men and women of those countries to go abroad and study.

Also, if the U.N. experts plan a big electric-power dam in Burma, and if enough Burmese study and learn how to build it, the U.N. International Bank lends the money.

That way the dam can really be built. The people can run it themselves. The electricity will power new factories. In the factories the people can make shoes, blankets, plows. Then the whole country becomes less poor.

The U.N. has been spending twenty million dollars a year on this technical-aid program (not counting the loans). The money has come from fifty-five countries. Sixty-four countries have received the aid. A U.N. committee manages it, and all the specialized agencies do parts of the work.

Has that been enough? In May, 1951, a group of U.N. experts studied this question. They reported that seven hundred times that much would be needed to raise the standard of living in the underdeveloped countries at all—say, two per cent a year.

In spite of everything the U.N. had been able to do, the poor nations were becoming poorer and worse off, not better.

Probably the most important thing the U.N. has ever done has been to discover this fact.

The U.N. also discovered that in 1951 more than half the people in the world could not read or write. Do you think that might be one of the reasons why they were so poor?

In the village of Pátzcuaro beside a pleasant, quiet lake in Mexico an Indian sat at a desk. His eyes looked out eagerly under black bushy eyebrows. With one arm he held his little boy, in the other hand a book. The man's heavy moustache waggled as he slowly read the words.

It is thrilling to watch the joy in the faces of grown men and women who for the first time are learning to read.

In May, 1951, UNESCO opened a special school there. A hundred young teachers-in-training go every semester. They travel from many Latin-American countries and study how to teach adults to read and write.

It's not easy. Many tribes of Indians in the jungles of Brazil speak languages that have never been written. Many Africans and Asians speak little languages, each known to only about a hundred thousand people, languages that have never had any alphabets.

The teachers must first invent an alphabet for each language. Then they begin writing and printing the first books ever made in those languages.

Often it seems best, while teaching those people to read, to teach them at the same time how to speak the national language. (In Brazil it's Portuguese.)

Experience has already shown another bad problem. After some of these people have been taught, they are too poor to buy any books or newspapers. So they soon forget how to read.

The teachers and students at the UNESCO center at Pátzcuaro began preparing books. Books about what? They believe that people need to learn about how to stay healthy, about what kinds of food are best to eat, about the weather and the soil and good methods of farming, about arithmetic, and about their own country's laws and how their government is run.

UNESCO cannot pay for books on all these subjects,

but it prepares the books. The governments of the various countries can print them.

UNESCO decided to open a school in Egypt, two in Equatorial Africa, one in Asia Minor, one in India, and two in the Far East, teaching teachers how to teach illiterates.

UNESCO got the help of several colleges and science clubs in Boston and built a portable science museum. They sent it to Havana, to Quito, to Lima. At Lima in Peru it created a traffic jam in front of the National Library, as five thousand visitors a day crowded to see it.

The people saw pictures and model gadgets to demonstrate some basic truths of science, with full explanations printed in Spanish. They saw a gyroscope spinning and were invited to try to push it over. They watched a portable planetarium that showed how the stars move.

There was a reason for this exhibit. Factories in Latin America could not find enough trained workers for their laboratories. Most Latin-Americans have not been much interested in science. Consequently not enough people studied to be engineers. UNESCO tried to stir up some interest, to show what wonders the science student can find.

The Children's Republic at Moulin-Vieux (that means "old mill") in the Isère Valley in France began in 1949 with UNESCO's help. It gave homes to war orphans, juvenile delinquents, and refugee children.

In their printing shop the boys published their own newspaper. The children elected their officers and took responsibility for running the village.

In Korea UNESCO helped reopen schools destroyed by the war. The world organization was able to get money, books, and even toys from many private organizations.

A teacher or a research worker in Europe who needed books and scientific apparatus could not buy them from the United States because he was not allowed to send money out of his country. But now he can buy UNESCO coupons, and with these he can get his books and apparatus. Twenty-six countries accepted the coupon system.

Many schoolteachers, scientists, and engineers are grateful to UNESCO for the good work it has done in collecting information about better ways to run a school and about new scientific research.

Every year it publishes a book called *Study Abroad,* which tells high-school and college students where they can get fellowships that pay young people to study in other countries. (You can write a letter to UNESCO, United Nations, New York, and ask how you can get that book.)

Do people have a right to eat? Do people have a right to learn to read? What rights do people have?

A farmer tried to buy a field in California on which

to grow cabbages and cucumbers. But the police told him he was not allowed to own land. He was a foreigner.

Other foreigners own land. A Frenchman can buy a farm in Massachusetts. Swedes grow beets in their own fields in Minnesota. But a 1920 law in California said no Japanese could own land.

So the farmer went and asked a judge. The United States Appellate Court decided on April 24, 1950, that the California law was null and void because it was contrary to the U.N. Charter.

The U.N. Charter has been officially accepted by the United States and is law. It says we will respect human rights and fundamental freedoms for all people. And the right to buy and possess land in a community where other people do is a fundamental freedom.

Now the Japanese farmer is plowing his own field in California just like anybody else.

When any state law contradicts the U.N. Charter, the state law is ended. But this won't happen until somebody goes to court and proves it in the case of each law. People might do this in several parts of the United States.

As the Charter was a little vague about human rights, the U.N. set up a committee to study the subject. With Mrs. Franklin D. Roosevelt serving on it, the committee held many meetings and consulted thousands of people.

Gradually they wrote a six-page Declaration of Human Rights. December 10, 1948, the U.N. General Assembly voted on it. Forty-eight nations voted for it, none against.

That made it official, and immediately it began to have some effect.

It gave the various councils and committees of the U.N. a common standard to guide them. The great specialized agencies shifted their programs to help more toward the achievement of those rights.

Five nations soon wrote new constitutions. In Indonesia, Syria, Costa Rica, El Salvador, and Haiti the new basic laws included sections patterned from the U.N. Declaration of Human Rights.

Ontario in Canada passed a Fair Employment Practices Act, quoting the U.N. declaration that people of all races and religions have the right to work.

In Washington the American Federation of Labor went to court when it attempted to force men to join a union. The A.F. of L. lost the case because the United States Supreme Court upheld the U.N. declaration that "No one may be compelled to belong to an association."

The U.N. signed an agreement allowing Italy to govern Somaliland for ten years in trusteeship. Italy had to promise to give the natives the rights named in the U.N. declaration.

The peace treaty with Japan in 1951 made Japan promise to give its own people those rights.

Still the courts in some countries—for example,

Austria and The Netherlands—refused to accept the declaration. They said it was not really law.

So the U.N. set to work to write treaties or covenants on human rights. If the General Assembly agrees, it will ask all the nations to accept them. This will help, because a treaty is more than a declaration. Once a treaty has been officially accepted it really is law.

Do people have a right to be healthy?

In India eight young men in white work-clothes squatted in a half circle in a village street. They were local health department workers. They stared at half a dozen buckets and hand pumps and some cans of insect poison. Two men, trained by the World Health Organization and the United Nations International Children's Emergency Fund, showed how to use these in fighting malaria mosquitoes.

A young Haitian mother brought her baby, two years old, for a penicillin injection to cure it of yaws. The woman wore a kerchief over her head and a straw hat on top of that. Her eyes showed her fear of white man's magic, but she was going to try it.

A nurse, sent by WHO, explained to her that the jab of the needle might make the baby cry, but the terrible disease would be ended.

In Iran whole villages lost their crops and starved. This happened often. At harvest time most of the workers were sick with malaria. The few who were well enough to go into the fields could gather only a tiny fraction of the grain. The same tragedy happened again and again in Yugoslavia, in Greece, in Pakistan.

Iran's government appealed to the U.N. for help. In the spring of 1950, WHO began a seven-year plan for malaria control. Spraying teams covered seventy million square miles with DDT and sprayed 440,000 houses.

In Pakistan a whole valley was sprayed. During the next two years nobody lost a single hour of work from malaria. The next valley was not sprayed, and half the population lost at least two weeks a year. (That's not so bad if the weeks don't come at harvest or planting, but usually they do.)

In Yugoslavia, Greece, Iran, and Pakistan the crop yield of the whole country increased fifteen per cent merely because the farmers were standing up instead of lying down.

In France and Italy tuberculosis hit less than half as many children in 1949 as it had in 1941. WHO and UNICEF had been busy with X-rays and inoculations.

In 1950 WHO received a letter which said it was from "the common people of Indonesia."

> *We want to tell you that already thousands of our people who were sick, now are well. And we wish we could show you the joy of mothers watching their children play without more suffering. We wish to thank you for the*

part you have played in restoring the miracle
of health to the long-suffering people. We ask
that WHO continue its work.

WHO does not have enough money to be able to reach
many areas where malaria is still common. So the disease continues and will spread again.

But the organization gathers information. It sends
out pamphlets and bulletins. It hopes that governments
will use this knowledge and carry on the fight.

WHO particularly wants to beat malaria, tuberculosis, typhus, and a couple of other epidemic diseases.
With more money the organization could greatly reduce the prevalence of these epidemics.

The U.N. would also like to smash the narcotics
racket. Its opium committee has been carrying on the
League of Nations' work. By 1951 the committee had
plenty of information on where dope came from.

So it began writing a plan by which the U.N. could
control the entire world supply. Opium would go only
to hospitals and doctors who use it for operations and
for medical cures.

When the U.N. was only six years old it had already
accomplished a lot of international working together
for people who were poor, ignorant, hungry, or sick.
The U.N. had already done more of this than any international organization before.

One reason why it has done more than the League of

Nations is that the U.N. has had more money. The politicians learned that it could handle money well. So the nations began to give it large sums. Together they vote how much it will spend, and what fraction each country will give.

The other reason is that men and women have learned more about how to run a world organization. They have discovered more and more of what this great new gadget can do.

Does the U.N. seem perfect? Maybe we still have more to learn and more to discover about what a world organization could do.

15. *Some Countries Do Not Govern Themselves*

BEFORE 1776 most of North and South America were governed by England, Spain, and Portugal.

But many people in thirteen of the colonies of North America objected. They disliked the laws and taxes decided by the English Parliament when Americans could not elect men to Parliament. Those laws forbade Americans to make and sell many things. The Americans wanted to elect their own governors and legislatures, which then would decide American laws and taxes.

So they fought a war and became independent.

By 1900 England, though it had lost the United States, had gained Australia, New Zealand, and India. Spain and Portugal had lost South America, but England, France, Belgium, and Germany had gained control of most of Africa. The Netherlands had most of the East Indies.

That meant that a great many people—nearly half the population of the world—lived in countries that did not govern themselves.

But that soon changed again.

By 1950 Canada, Australia, New Zealand, the Union of South Africa, and India (divided into India and Pakistan) were no longer colonies. They had become self-governing dominions of the British Commonwealth of Nations. They could elect their own parliaments and make their own laws.

Other colonies were gaining their freedom, too.

The United Nations inherited the old League's mandates system. But time and war had made some changes.

Five non-Turkish countries carved from the former Turkish Empire were mandated in 1919 to Great Britain and France. But they began to struggle for independence.

Iraq became free in 1932. During World War II Lebanon achieved independence. After the war the other three followed in quick succession: Trans-Jordan, then Syria, then Palestine.

What has been happening? Since 1932 the whole system of colonies has been fading out. In 1945 to 1950 —the first five years after World War II—a quarter of the world's population became independent (counting India and Indonesia).

That still left about 120,000,000 people in non-self-governing areas (mostly in Africa).

The former German colonies in Africa were mandated in 1919 to Great Britain, France, Belgium, and the Union of South Africa.

Forty years later these had all become trust territories under the watchful eyes of the United Nations—with one exception.

The exception was South West Africa. The Union of South Africa passed a law during World War II saying that this area would be part of the Union. Did this mean the people there became self-governing? Delegates of many nations in the U.N. said no, and they had a lot of fun scolding the Union of South Africa about this.

German colonies in the Pacific Ocean were divided up in 1919. New Zealand, Australia, and Great Britain got three groups of the islands. Japan got the rest.

Forty years later these were all trust territories under

the watchful eyes of the U.N.—with only one change.

The batch of islands formerly mandated to Japan (Mariana, Caroline, and Marshall islands) are now entrusted to the United States.

Crowds of Negroes stood on both sides of the street, cheering and waving flags. Half a dozen jeeps paraded through the town. On each fender were painted the letters "U.N."

The police officers in the jeeps were the U.N.'s own field-service men. Several hundred of these men, carefully trained at U.N. headquarters in New York, are out all the time protecting U.N. committees in many countries.

The crowds were glad because a U.N. commissioner had arrived to help write a constitution for Eritrea in Africa. For three generations the Eritreans had been an Italian colony. In 1941 they had been conquered by a British army. The people, by race and language, were close cousins of the Ethiopians.

The U.N. commissioner riding in one of the jeeps (Señor Matienzo of Bolivia) brought along lawyers and interpreters to help him. During the next few weeks he consulted the Eritrean Assembly and the emperor of Ethiopia. Then he wrote a constitution, making sure it was one they would accept. It also had to be one the U.N. General Assembly would accept. His instructions from the U.N. were to make it democratic and to put

in guarantees to protect the personal rights and freedoms of the Eritreans.

Actually the new constitution was a success. It was
accepted. And in 1951 Eritrea became a state in Ethiopia
(like New Jersey in the United States).

This all happened because the United States, Great
Britain, France, and the Soviet Union had signed a
treaty saying that if they could not agree what to do with
Italy's colonies, these four big countries would dump
the problem on the U.N. General Assembly.

Of course they could not agree. So the General
Assembly rolled up its sleeves, smiling, and went to
work. At last it was acting as a real legislature. Its decisions would be final.

After settling Eritrea's fate, the Assembly decided
to make Libya an independent nation. Libya will have
hard going, because it is very large, with very few
people, and their income has averaged about twenty-
five dollars a year per person. Anyway, they became a
separate, free nation December 24, 1951.

The U.N. General Assembly gave Italian Somaliland back to Italy, but with strings attached. The colony
became a trust territory. It is run by Italy—with the
help (rather annoying help, probably) of delegates from
Egypt, the Philippine Islands, and the Republic of
Colombia.

Italy has promised to give the Somali people full
personal rights and freedoms. The U.N. keeps asking

questions and sending investigators in jeeps full
of field-service men to see that Italy behaves herself
there.

And all this is for only ten years. In 1960 Italian
Somaliland is to become an independent nation.

Almost eighteen million people are living in the
dozen U.N. trust territories. More might come in. Some
officials in the Egyptian Sudan, for example, said they
would like to try it.

The U.N. system works a lot better than the old
League of Nations system did. The main weakness used
to be that the League could not find out what was being
done in the mandated colonies. It had no jeeps, no
field-service men, and no legal right to go and look.

Now the U.N. sends a regular visiting committee
once a year to tour some of the trust territories. The
committee enters them all at least once every three
years. When the colonial people see those jeeps coming,
they feel they have not been forgotten. And all year
round the U.N. flag flies over government offices in the
territories.

In 1947 the people of Western Samoa sent a petition
to the U.N. saying, "We want to become free and independent."

A special U.N. committee went there and looked and
asked questions.

The committee decided that the Samoans were not
ready to run their country alone. But the U.N. said the

French ought to let the Samoan people elect more of their own local officers, like mayors of towns.

The U.N. Trusteeship Council also scolded Belgium and recommended that the Belgians could do better in Ruanda-Urundi, in Africa. The tax system should be improved. Wages could be raised. And they ought to stop whipping people in the jails.

The U.N. Security Council nudged the United States about its trust islands in the Pacific. The natives ought to have more share in the government.

Even as recently as forty or fifty years ago no world organization could have scolded sovereign nations like this. They would have felt insulted, ready to fight.

But now we smile (or frown) and accept it. This means that we are gradually becoming accustomed to world organization. We are gradually giving it more power.

What about the rest of the non-self-governing areas?

The United States has several: Alaska, Hawaii, Puerto Rico, and a lot of small islands. Great Britain and France still have a great many colonies, mostly in Africa.

A little over 100,000,000 people live in these places. Some of them vote for local officers. But they don't have any say in big things: national taxes, military doings, tariffs.

When the League of Nations was arguing at Geneva, many hundreds of millions of people lived in non-self-governing colonies. But the League never even tried to do anything for them.

The U.N. has been poking its big sharp nose into every colony in the world (and has found some bad smells).

Somebody had the bright idea of writing into the U.N. Charter a whole page of noble ideals about colonies. Somehow the big nations that run colonies never quite had the nerve to cut that out. It is still in the Charter.

In that page (Articles 73 and 74) those big nations promise to be good and to take care of the colonial people. They also promise to send information to the U.N. about all the non-self-governing colonies.

The U.N. General Assembly has often smacked its lips eagerly over that page in the Charter. Sixty nations vote in the Assembly, and only eight of them have colonies. Right away in 1946 the Assembly asked for that promised information.

The nations that had colonies sent a few facts—mostly statistics that were not very interesting.

The Assembly complained. The delegates wanted more. They voted to have the Secretariat send out a long questionnaire.

Some of the nations that had colonies became angry. Their delegates made indignant speeches. They said it was none of the U.N.'s business to poke its nose into colonies.

But the United States shrugged its shoulders and told the Assembly to go ahead. Why not? The United States is no good at keeping secrets anyway. The newspapers in Puerto Rico, for instance, can print whatever they please. The delegates of nineteen nations in the U.N. who read Spanish can read them. What good would it do the United States to try to hide any of the facts about Puerto Rico?

So the Assembly voted to put even more questions in the U.N. questionnaire.

The result is that the U.N. is collecting more and more information about all colonies. It learns how many schools each colony has, how many teachers, how many pupils, how much money is spent on schools (not very much). It learns how many colonial people are sick, and how much food they have to eat (not enough). It learns whether any progress is being made in giving them more control over their own local governments. (The people are getting more control. Actually a lot of progress is being made.)

Then the Assembly votes its recommendations. It does not yet have any power over colonies outside its own trust areas. But it can raise a loud yell. And it does.

16. *The U.N. Tries to Keep Peace*

WHAT HAS the U.N. done to prevent war?

In April, 1947, the British government announced that it was tired of trying to govern Palestine and would dump that country's problems on the U.N.

So the General Assembly went to work. It sent a U.N. committee to find out the facts. When the committee came back, the General Assembly voted that Palestine should be divided into two states, Arab and Jewish. Jerusalem should be under international control. The U.N. drew a map, showing the proposed boundary between the two states.

The British departed from Palestine suddenly.

On May 14, 1948, the Jews announced that they were a new nation called Israel, accepting the boundary drawn by the U.N.

But the Arabs objected. Immediately all the neighboring Arab countries marched their soldiers in and began fighting against the new Israeli nation.

The Jews fought back. They fought hard. They drove the Arabs out of the country entirely and even moved its boundaries, making Israel larger. They took Jerusalem and made it their capital.

The U.N. passed resolutions, ordering both sides to stop fighting. But the war continued. Even after the Jews had won, the Arabs kept on fighting a little around the edges of the country and sent an airplane once in a while to drop bombs on Jewish cities.

The U.N. sent a committee to try to arrange a peace agreement between the two sides. The committee was led by Count Folke Bernadotte of the royal family of Sweden.

Count Bernadotte was murdered by Jewish extremists.

Ralph Bunche became head of the committee. He

bravely continued the negotiations with both Arabs and Jews in spite of threats and violence around him.

The U.N. mission to Palestine was no Sunday School picnic. Dr. Bunche spent $750,000 a month. He commanded over seven hundred military observers and civilian representatives from more than thirty nations. He had sixteen airplanes, hundreds of trucks and jeeps, three destroyers, and a French corvette.

He persuaded both sides to promise to make a temporary truce. They promised several times, and both sides often violated the truce by shooting at each other again.

Nevertheless he continued. Little by little he worked out a treaty which both sides would accept. At last in February, 1949, he got them to sign a general armistice, which ended the fighting.

Next year Dr. Bunche was awarded the Nobel Peace Prize for his bravery and patience and tact. He was the first American Negro ever to receive the Nobel Peace Prize.

Eighty million people live in Java, Sumatra, and nearby islands. They have brown skins, and most of them are Mohammedans.

The islands used to be divided into several colonies governed by the Netherlands. They were called the Netherlands East Indies or the Dutch East Indies. And they were extremely rich in rubber plants, coffee, tea, tobacco and also tin, oil, and coal. But the people were extremely poor.

During World War II the Japanese conquered the whole area. It was a valuable prize.

When the Japanese surrendered at the end of the war, the Dutch were very eager to get it back. They sent in a few soldiers to take control.

But the Indonesian people wanted to govern themselves. Many revolted. Their leaders chose a president and a parliament and announced that they were a new nation, the Indonesian Republic.

The Dutch bought a lot of guns and sent an army to Indonesia. They also got sixty thousand British soldiers to help. War raged over the vast expanse of the many islands, and blood wet the earth of the rubber and coffee plantations.

In the U.N. the delegates from Australia and India demanded that the Security Council take action.

The Council sent a committee, which went in a ship of the United States Navy all the way to Java. After a lot of talk the U.N. committee persuaded both sides to sign an agreement. The Dutch promised to respect the Indonesian Republic. Together the new nation and The Netherlands would be a union, having the same queen. In March, 1947, this became official.

A year later the Dutch were fighting again. They conquered most of the islands, captured the leaders of the republic, including the president, and put them in jail. The Dutch began to make the whole region a colony again.

The Security Council met immediately. Its committee reported that the Dutch had broken the agreement.

The Security Council voted and sent a telegram to the Dutch, ordering them to stop the shooting and to set free the leaders of the Indonesian Republic.

The Dutch refused to do either of these things.

The Security Council met again. What should it do? It could ask all the nations to make war against the Dutch. It could ask all the nations merely to boycott the Dutch.

The delegates decided that first they would try using the pressure of public opinion. They passed several resolutions saying the Dutch were in the wrong.

Then the Council waited. Would this method work?

Delegates from the governments of Australia, India, and all the other Asiatic countries near Indonesia met in India. They voted to support the Indonesian Republic against the Dutch.

This meeting had no legal power. It only expressed the opinion of some large governments.

At that time the United States had begun sending large quantities of money and weapons to most European countries. In the spring of 1949 the United States Congress voted to stop sending any of this help to The

Netherlands unless The Netherlands would obey the Security Council.

That is what is called the pressure of public opinion.

Right away the Dutch sent telegrams to the U.N. saying they were only working for peace. Meaning what?

The U.N. committee went to The Hague (the capital of The Netherlands) to find out. They sat at a long table. On one side were some Dutch officials. On the other side were the Indonesian leaders, fresh out of jail.

The U.N. committee looked very hard and very coldly into the eyes of both sides. After a good deal of talk and a great deal of help from the U.N. gentlemen, a new agreement was written. The Republic of Indonesia was to be a real nation, governing itself immediately. The Netherlands and Indonesia together would have the same queen.

This time the agreement worked. The Indonesian leaders hurried home and began organizing the various islands of their enormous country into one nation.

December 27, 1949, the Queen of The Netherlands signed a proclamation making it official. That day in Jakarta in Java, President Soekarno stood at a microphone on a platform before a crowd of his people and took the oath of office.

Many Dutch people who had left Indonesia during the fighting came back again. Soon over a hundred thousand of them were living peacefully in the islands.

In 1950 Indonesia was admitted to the U.N., becoming the sixtieth member. Her delegate stood up before the General Assembly and thanked the U.N. for its work. He said the U.N. had "introduced the spirit of conciliation and reason" into the discussions between his people and the Dutch.

World War II ended when the emperor of Japan ordered all his soldiers to surrender. In Korea, American soldiers landed in the south, and Russian soldiers marched in from the north. Wherever they found any Japanese soldiers, the Americans and Russians collected all their guns, bullets, jeeps, tanks, airplanes, and marched the men away.

To the Koreans this was amazing. Their country had been occupied by the Japanese for forty years. The principal of every school was a Japanese, and the only language taught was Japanese. The old Korean language and its ancient culture had been pushed aside. And half the people could not read or write.

Hurriedly the United States commanders agreed with the Russians that in Korea American soldiers would accept the surrender of the Japanese south of the thirty-eighth parallel (an invisible line, which existed only on the maps) and Russian soldiers would accept the surrender of the Japanese north of that line.

This was done.

Meanwhile President Roosevelt and Marshall Stalin

had signed an agreement that after the war Korea should become an independent country.

This was not done.

Instead the Russians made the thirty-eighth parallel an iron curtain. They would not allow anyone to enter and see what they were doing in North Korea. For three years they occupied it and built up a powerful North Korean army, equipped with captured Japanese weapons and also some from Russia. Naturally they set up a communist government there.

The United States presented a formal complaint to the U.N. in 1947 that—contrary to the treaty—Korea was still divided in two.

The General Assembly voted to send a committee with instructions to do three things. The committee would go to Korea, tour the whole country, and get the facts. All foreign soldiers were to leave Korea, and the U.N. committee would watch them go. Also the U.N. committee would order elections to be held in the whole country.

The committee went to Korea. But the communists would not allow it to enter the northern part of the country.

The committee ordered elections to be held. This was done in South Korea. But the committee made the mistake of believing that it should not interfere with Korea's local affairs. So it allowed the Korean politicians to manage the elections. A lot of cheating was done at the polls, and the government that was elected was not very popular.

The committee then suggested that all foreign soldiers should leave the country and let the Koreans run it themselves.

This was done. The United States soldiers departed, while the U.N. committee watched. The Russian soldiers also departed from North Korea, although they would not let the committee come and watch.

But a treaty had been broken, and the U.N. had been defied. The country was still divided into two parts.

The delegates in the U.N. General Assembly decided that this situation was dangerous. So they told their committee to stay there and keep watching.

During five years of freedom the Korean schools improved. Most people learned to read and write. The number of children in schools in South Korea increased greatly. The communists also made similar progress in North Korea.

At four o'clock in the morning on June 25, 1950, North Korean soldiers swarmed across the artificial border into South Korea. They captured a few South Korean soldiers. Any who resisted were shot, except those who hid and shot back. Soon a battle was raging, with many killed on both sides.

The U.N. committee got out of bed, hurriedly made telephone calls, spent seven hours gathering the facts, and radioed a report direct to the U.N. headquarters in

New York. They said the attack was an aggression, an attempt to grab South Korea.

In the days when Emeric Crucé and Jean Jacques Rousseau were writing plans for a world organization to keep peace, they worried about what would happen when the soldiers of one country attacked another. A messenger on horseback would ride to the port and get in a sailboat. To go from Korea to New York he would take at least six months. What could the Security Council do then?

But in 1950 the message went in a few seconds. At last men had radios, telephones, and airplanes with which to run a world organization. Only one question remained. Was the organization designed right, so that it could prevent one country from grabbing another?

Dates and time in Korea are fourteen hours ahead of New York. By New York time the attack began at 2:00 P.M. on June 24. The U.N. committee's message reached New York at 9:00 P.M. Clerks in the U.N. headquarters began telephoning all the offices of the delegates of the eleven nations that were members of the Security Council.

As it was Saturday, many of the men were out of town. President Truman was in Missouri. The communists had chosen that moment on purpose. But maybe the communists did not realize that President Truman could consult all his advisers instantly by telephone.

At half-past two next afternoon, Sunday, the Security

Council met. The delegates had already had time to discuss the problem with their advisers. They were ready to act. And they did.

Only ten were present. It so happened that Russia was at that time boycotting the Security Council. So the Russian delegate was not there to use his veto.

The Council voted that the attack was a breach of the peace. That means that it was a crime, and police action could be taken against the aggressors.

The Council sent a cablegram to the government of North Korea, inviting it to withdraw its soldiers from South Korea. Many years before, the League of Nations had invited Greece to withdraw its soldiers from Bulgaria, and Greece actually did.

Finally the Council also voted to ask all the countries in the entire United Nations to "give every assistance" to the U.N. in putting these decisions into effect.

That evening President Truman studied these words. To "give every assistance"? How much should he do? He cabled to General MacArthur in Japan, authorizing him to give weapons and bullets to South Korea.

For two days Truman and his advisers watched the news from Korea. The fight was continuing. The North Korean communist army was disobeying the Security Council and was fighting its way deeper into South Korea. Then a message came from the government of South Korea, saying, "Please send real help!"

Years before, Japan had defied the League of Nations.

Italy had defied the League of Nations. So the League perished, and there was nothing to prevent World War II.

If the North Koreans were allowed to defy the Security Council, other countries soon would do the same. The U.N. would perish, and there would be nothing to prevent World War III.

At noon on June 27 President Truman announced that he was ordering airplanes and battleships to go and help the South Korean army.

That afternoon the Security Council met again. The Russian delegate still was absent.

The men in the Council discussed Korea. They decided that airplanes and battleships were not enough. More help would be needed. The Council voted to ask all countries in the entire United Nations to send "such assistance to the Republic of Korea as may be necessary to repel the armed attack and to restore international peace and security in the area."

Within a few days American soldiers began to fight side by side with the South Koreans. As soon as they could, soldiers from other nations joined them. Sixteen nations sent armies. Five more nations sent doctors, nurses, and equipment for field hospitals.

Other nations sent money, medicines, food, clothes. Fifty-three nations announced their support of the U.N. fight against aggression in Korea.

According to its Charter the United Nations was to

have had an army. Every nation would keep some forces ready. Some countries would keep airplanes, others submarines, others only soldiers with machine guns, and so on. Naturally this must be carefully planned, so that all these forces could act immediately if the Security Council should send out its call. And naturally the Big Five nations would have the largest forces ready.

So the military chiefs of staff of the Big Five nations were to have met together and made the plans.

Actually they had met. They had argued. The Russians had not agreed to any of the plans. After two years of talk, the military committee had simply stopped meeting. And therefore when the Korean War started, there was no U.N. army. After the war began, the U.N. gathered an army together.

Consequently at first they had trouble. The U.N. troops retreated before the attack of the North Koreans, who conquered most of the country.

But at last enough U.N. soldiers and guns arrived. They pushed the North Koreans back almost all the way to the border of Manchuria. They planned to hold elections in all Korea at once, as the U.N. General Assembly had directed.

But at the moment before a U.N. victory, the armies of the Chinese communists marched into Korea in such large numbers that they drove the U.N. troops back again.

The U.N. General Assembly discussed this attack by

the Chinese. The Assembly voted that the Chinese were aggressors, and announced that the U.N. would continue its action to stop the aggression.

The U.N. was not going to die from sheer weakness, as the League of Nations had done. At last an international organization was strong enough to use force.

17. *How We Can End War*

THE UNITED NATIONS has been trying to keep peace—whenever possible—by talk. The U.N. has recommended a cease-fire or a new boundary line, and hoped the quarreling nations would accept it. More often the U.N. has sent a committee to listen to both sides and gradually write a treaty they would accept.

The United Nations has tried to keep peace also by force. This is new. No world organization ever tried it before. When the leaders of a country defy the U.N.

and send soldiers with big guns, tanks, and airplanes to make war, the U.N. can reply with soldiers, big guns, tanks, and airplanes supplied by many countries.

These can be sent, says the U.N. Charter, by the Security Council. When the Korean War began, the Russians happened to be boycotting the Council. But that mistake taught them a lesson. After that they sent a delegate to all meetings.

If another communist country starts a war, the Russian delegate will certainly be at the long curved table and will veto whatever the Council tries to do.

What can the other delegates do then? Must they be helpless?

For many centuries nations have been slowly learning how to work together. International organization grew all the way from the Telegraph Union in 1865, through the Postal Union and the League of Nations, to the much larger United Nations in only eighty years.

The U.N., too, is changing and growing. It has already got around the veto.

The General Assembly in 1950 voted that in case of war, if the Security Council is stopped by a veto, the General Assembly will meet. Normally the Assembly meets only once a year for three or four months. But now the delegates can be called together at any time. They need only twenty-four hours' notice.

The Assembly also created the necessary committees. They are ready to go into action quickly. When they do, the Assembly will have all the powers that the Council has. It can order a world-wide boycott against an aggressor nation. Or it can call out the soldiers if necessary.

And in the Assembly no nation has any veto. Decisions are made by two-thirds majority.

The U.N. is growing in other ways, too. More nations are joining. Many more may join—including Germany and Japan. It will be truly a world organization when former enemies are in.

If the leaders of some nation start a war, must the U.N. send bullets and bombs against that whole nation? This use of force is new. Maybe we are not yet doing it the best way. Couldn't the U.N. send police to arrest only the guilty leaders?

The U.N.'s International Law Commission (twelve experts appointed by the General Assembly) studied these questions. They reported, "Crimes against international law are committed by men." Crimes, such as starting a war, are not committed, they said, by a whole nation. And the U.N. can keep peace "only by punishing individuals who commit such crimes."

In December, 1950, the U.N. General Assembly accepted this idea. The Assembly appointed a committee to plan an international criminal court. This court will try men who start wars or who even plan to begin a war.

But first some authority must make laws for this court to enforce. Who will make the laws?

Mr. Trygve Lie, the first Secretary-General of the U.N., said the U.N. should do it. In 1950 he traveled to London, Paris, Moscow, and Washington. He discussed this plan with the leading officials.

Fifty years previously the idea would have sounded like a beautiful but impossible dream. But times have changed. The delegates of most of the nations in the world, meeting in the U.N. General Assembly, voted for a committee to work on it.

For centuries the nations have been slowly learning to do more and more together.

The United States, which never joined the League of Nations, is now in the U.N. The United States has also become more and more active in the Organization of American States (Pan American Union) and in the North Atlantic Treaty Organization (NATO), sending money and guns for a European army.

The United States receives ambassadors from more than seventy governments and sends its ambassadors to those countries. The United States also has day-to-day contact with those governments' representatives in the U.N. And money, people, books, movies, and merchandise go from the United States to those countries and from them to the United States. More than ever before.

Also millions of United States citizens have friendships or do business with men and women all over the world. Business companies open more mines and factories and sales offices abroad. Schools and colleges send more and more students on traveling fellowships. More ships and airplanes take more tourists. Each year sees another increase in the vast quantity of international mail. And newspapers, radios, magazines, and books keep us informed of happenings abroad.

In all these ways our nation is becoming more connected to the world.

The same thing is happening to all other nations. Even the countries behind the Iron Curtain, though separated from the Western world, are becoming more closely connected to one another.

While co-operation among countries has been growing rapidly, like a large-boned, healthy young man, something else has been growing too. War.

Ever since war was invented by the apes, it has become steadily worse. More people have been killed, more people wounded. More houses, food, clothes have been destroyed. More money is spent on weapons. More time is spent by more men in preparing for war and in fighting.

War probably will continue to grow worse. If we don't stop it, it will take a larger part of our money and time, destroy more cities, kill and wound a larger proportion of the population.

The Third World War, with atom bombs, will be much worse than the Second. The Fourth will be worse than the Third. And so on.

Now the two great growing giants, like two huge angry men, are nearly ready for their final head-on collision. Co-operation among the countries stands on one side. War on the other. They both will keep on growing bigger and bigger and stronger and stronger, until one destroys the other forever.

War was invented by the great tailless apes. It will be stopped by educated, thinking people. By you, perhaps.

What powers must we add to the U.N. for it to become strong enough to stop war?

The delegates in the General Assembly have not been elected by the people. The United States President appoints the delegates for the United States. The government of each nation appoints its own.

Could they make laws? Do you think that real laws, which people must obey, should be made by delegates who have not been elected by the people?

We elect the men and women in our city council, in our state legislature, in our nation's Congress. If we elected our representatives to the U.N., couldn't we let them make laws, too?

In the General Assembly each nation now has one vote. El Salvador with two million people has one vote.

Indonesia with eighty million people has one vote. The United States with 155,000,000 people has one vote. So these votes do not represent the people.

How should this be changed, if the U.N. is to have real power and make laws to jail men who scheme for war?

In order to stop war the U.N. might take command over all soldiers. Each country would keep merely a police force with which to catch robbers and manage mobs. Only the U.N. would have any army.

The United States Government has urged that only the U.N. should control atomic energy. The U.N. should see to it that atomic energy is used for electricity and to heat houses, not for bombs.

If the U.N. could regulate world trade, it could help the poor countries to stop becoming poorer. If the U.N. could set minimum-wage standards everywhere, the rich countries would at last be protected against unfair competition by cheap foreign labor.

Many people have said the U.N. should not allow any iron curtain. If the U. N. had power, it should make laws that any book, newspaper, or magazine that tells the truth may go anywhere in the world. Then any person who behaves himself will be allowed to go, too, anywhere in the world and take his money with him.

That is about all that's needed to stop war.

The U.N. must not interfere in local affairs. Every state or town ought to keep its right to make its own laws about robbery, murder, gambling, liquor, divorce, and the censorship of comic books. The people of each country must keep the right to decide for themselves what languages their country will use, what economic system it will encourage, what political methods it will be governed by.

Many of the government leaders in the world agree that that stronger U.N., having real powers, could at last prevent war.

The method has been growing for nearly a hundred years. It is becoming stronger, as the U.N. gets more power. Do you want it soon to become strong enough?

That is not the end of the story of how countries get along with one another.

At first that stronger U.N., with elected delegates, will probably not be very good. We shall need to work hard to improve it.

For instance, it ought to have a world bill of rights, enforced by U.N. courts, guaranteeing personal freedoms to everyone everywhere, not only in your own country. But you may have to study, think, and talk and vote many times in order to achieve world-wide freedom.

When the U.N. has become strong enough we shall no longer have to waste our time, our money, our thought, blood, and suffering, on war. War, invented by apes, is stupid. It is boring. The future, with its new tasks, can be far more interesting.

First we may learn what to do for the many people who are starving or poor or sick or who cannot read.

And, as long as men, women, and children live, they will always keep changing their governments, their schools, their modern painting, their ways of doing business. Some changes are great improvements. Some are not. Most changes begin with arguments. Often they cause hard feelings, sometimes real suffering for a few people.

There will always be plenty of struggles, plenty of trouble.

But some day—maybe soon—there will be no more war.

Index